A Christmas Drama Collection

Volume 1

Three Evangelistic Christmas Dramas

By Randy Pilz

"THE GREATEST LOVE"

"THE CHRISTMAS RUNAWAY"

"A SPECIAL ADAPTATION OF A CHRISTMAS CAROL"

These dramas are works of fiction. Although they are set during various periods of history, fictional characters and scenes from the author's imagination have been added to create a plausible story within the historical settings. Any resemblance to actual persons, living or dead, outside the historical accounts is coincidental.

The Scripture references are taken from the King James Version of the Bible or are paraphrased by the author based on that version.

All images used are either owned by the author or in the Public Domain available over the Internet.

You may contact the author at pilz.author@gmail.com

ISBN Information:
e-Book ISBN: 978-0-9997980-3-4
Paperback *ISBN: 978-0-9997980-2-7*

Contents

Author's Foreword

"The Greatest Love"

Production Notes for "The Greatest Love"

"The Christmas Runaway"

Production Notes for "The Christmas Runaway"

"A Christmas Carol"

Production Notes for "A Christmas Carol"

Tips for Actors

About the Author

Acknowledgements

FOREWORD

For many years I served as the drama director at Falls Baptist Church in Menomonee Falls, WI under the leadership of Pastor Wayne Van Gelderen, Jr.

After using a number of the cantatas and programs available through various sacred music publishers, I sought something new and began to write my own evangelistic dramas for use in our church. Because of our situation in Wisconsin, other denominations outnumber the independent Baptist churches. Many of these folks might not visit us for church services or evangelistic meetings. We sought to present bigger Christmas and Easter productions of music and drama which provided our church members outreach opportunities to invite their unsaved family, friends and co-workers to something outside our regular meetings. The dramas in this book are some of the results of those efforts.

Although works of fiction, these dramas strive to present the Word of God and the Gospel in an honest, compelling manner. Often based on an actual experience, the stories try to show how God might work through His Word in a person's life, bringing that person to salvation. Each story describes a conversion experience where at least one of the characters trusts Jesus Christ as his personal Savior.
It is my prayer that these dramas bless the hearts of those who read them, are a blessing to the churches, schools, and organizations that present them, and help lead lost souls to saving faith in the Lord Jesus Christ.

Sincerely,

Randy Pilz
Taylors, South Carolina

December 1944 - The Battle of the Bulge

THE GREATEST LOVE

BY
RANDY PILZ

*"Greater love hath no man than this,
that a man lay down his life for his friends."*
John 15:13

The Greatest Love

A Christmas Drama

"Greater Love Hath No Man Than This,
That He Lay Down His Life For His Friends"
John 15:13

By Randy Pilz

This story appears in an expanded form in the novel
A Battle More Desperate by Randy Pilz available at Amazon.com.

Dedication:
This drama is dedicated to
all the men and women in uniform
who were soldiers of the King of Kings
as well as soldiers of their country.

Introduction:

This Christmas drama represents years of researching, writing, and development. It was initially written to commemorate the 50th anniversary of the Battle of the Bulge in 1994, and has since been upgraded and re-edited.

Although the characters and situations in this story are fictional, great care was taken to make the historical setting as accurate as possible. Men like Joe Anderson and Wendell Burnanski did exist. The commemorative plaques that once hung in the War Memorial Chapel at Bob Jones University told of their sacrifice. After the war, the Preacher's Classes at schools like BJU swelled with the ranks of men returning from the war and preparing for full-time Christian service.

This program may be produced as a cantata-type program with choir music or as a straight drama. Suggested Music locations are indicated in the script. A complete list of music, along with suggestions on staging, costumes, etc., is included in the Production Notes at the end of this script.

This script has been newly adapted from the form used for the original production at Falls Baptist Church in Menomonee Falls, Wisconsin, in December 1994. Feel free to adapt it further to suit your own needs and circumstances.

Stage directions are in parentheses (*like this*), marked in italics. Staging suggestions are in the Production Notes.

This script is marked with sound effects cues as they were in the original Falls Baptist Church production. To keep it simple, we did not use every instance where sound effects might have gone. You can be creative and add more, if you wish. The sound cues we did use are marked with the designation **SFX**. Please feel free to alter or ignore any of these to suit your own production and circumstances. There are many standard sound effects available on on the Internet. A list of the sound effects is in the Production Notes at the end of this script.

If you produce this drama in your church or school, please notify the author and let him know how things went. You may e-mail him at pilz.author@gmail.com.

Characters

(In order of appearance)

NARRATOR 1: A Male narrator who also represents Wilcox's son or grandson decades later, depending on the age of the actor playing NARRATOR 1.

NARRATOR 2: A Female narrator who also plays MRS. ANDERSON, a middle-aged woman and born-again Christian. Concerned for her son, but trusting God to care for him.

NARRATOR 3: A Female narrator who also plays SUSAN ANDERSON, a young woman of late high school or early college age, and a born-again Christian, who worries for her older brother Joe.

WILCOX: A veteran paratrooper and squad leader, a history teacher in civilian life, keeps a journal.

SGT. REYNOLDS: A tough-as-nails, career army platoon sergeant.

COOPER: A veteran paratrooper, who likes to make wisecracks, constantly has a toothpick in his mouth.

LT. SMITH: A firm, no-nonsense platoon leader.

BURNANSKI: A hard case veteran paratrooper, looking for trouble, bitter and hurt from the loss of a close friend.

JOE ANDERSON: A new replacement, fresh from training; a former ministerial student who seeks to live for God and lead lost souls to the Savior wherever he is sent.

Note: An actual WWII squad at full strength would number 12 men. Three regular infantry squads and a weapons squad (heavy machine guns and mortars) would form a platoon. Because of recent losses in the Netherlands, the 101st Airborne at the time of the Battle of the Bulge was under strength and just begun the process of receiving and training replacements. For this drama, the SQUAD consists of WILCOX, COOPER, BURNANSKI, and ANDERSON. (In the novel based on this play, there are four additional men in the squad, two other veterans and two more replacements.) REYNOLDS and LT. SMITH join the SQUAD in the drama at certain times.

This program may be presented in two parts, as it premiered in 1994 at Falls Baptist Church. Part I features a package of Christmas Music performed by choirs and orchestra separate from the drama. Part II features the drama with appropriate choir music inserted. See the Production Notes at the end of this script for further music suggestions.

Part I: Christmas Music

(This part includes a short introductory reading to set the tone of the program)

MUSIC: MEN'S GROUP sings a capella "THE FIRST NOEL" up to the chorus (They continue humming the chorus and melody in the background until the NARRATORS are finished)

(*NARRATORS enter*)

NARRATOR 1: Love is the heart of the Christmas season.

NARRATOR 2: The time when we show others our love in the things we do, the songs we sing, and the gifts we give.

NARRATOR 3: A reflection of the love of God.

NARRATOR 2: God was the first and greatest one to show love at Christmas.

NARRATOR 1: Consider these words from the Gospel of John, chapter three, verse sixteen,

ALL: "For God so loved the world . . .

NARRATOR 2: . . . that He gave His only begotten son . . .

NARRATOR 1: . . . that whosoever believeth in Him should not perish. . .

NARRATOR 3: . . . but have everlasting life."

NARRATOR 2: The original Christmas love.

NARRATOR 1: God loves us.

NARRATOR 3: He sent His Son to be our Savior.

NARRATOR 2: Sacrificing Jesus Christ for others.

ALL: For us.

NARRATOR 3: The greatest giving.

NARRATOR 1: The greatest gift.

ALL: <u>THE GREATEST LOVE</u>!

(NARRATORS exit)

MUSIC: MEN'S GROUP: "THE FIRST NOEL"
(Pick up with the chorus and then sing the remaining verses.)

MUSIC: CHOIR PACKAGE (A package of Christmas carols not used in the drama. Our pastor wanted a lot of Christmas music in the program.

This included the children of the church. The Kindergarteners sang a simple song.

There were a lot of stings players of various levels starting with a Suzuki Strings Program on up. It is almost a tradition in that church that they play "O, Come Little Children."

Other children dressed in homemade costumes as angels, shepherds, wise men, The Inn Keeper, Mary and Joseph entered singing and stood across the platform and around the front of the church, forming a manger scene and sang another song.)

ANNOUNCEMENTS

OFFERTORY: Some sort of Instrumental Arrangement of Christmas music.

Characters

(In order of appearance)

NARRATOR 1: A Male narrator who also represents Wilcox's son or grandson decades later, depending on the age of the actor playing NARRATOR 1.

NARRATOR 2: A Female narrator who also plays MRS. ANDERSON, a middle-aged woman and born-again Christian. Concerned for her son, but trusting God to care for him.

NARRATOR 3: A Female narrator who also plays SUSAN ANDERSON, a young woman of late high school or early college age, and a born-again Christian, who worries for her older brother Joe.

WILCOX: A veteran paratrooper and squad leader, a history teacher in civilian life, keeps a journal.

SGT. REYNOLDS: A tough-as-nails, career army platoon sergeant.

COOPER: A veteran paratrooper, who likes to make wisecracks, constantly has a toothpick in his mouth.

LT. SMITH: A firm, no-nonsense platoon leader.

BURNANSKI: A hard case veteran paratrooper, looking for trouble, bitter and hurt from the loss of a close friend.

JOE ANDERSON: A new replacement, fresh from training; a former ministerial student who seeks to live for God and lead lost souls to the Savior wherever he is sent.

(An actual WWII squad at full strength would number 12 men. Three regular infantry squads and a weapons squad (heavy machine guns and mortars) would form a platoon. Because of recent losses in The Netherlands, the 101st Airborne at the time of the Battle of the Bulge was under strength and in the middle of receiving and training replacements. For this play the SQUAD consists of WILCOX, COOPER, BURNANSKI, and ANDERSON. [In the novel based on this play, there are four additional men in the squad, two other veterans and two more replacements.] REYNOLDS, and LT. SMITH join the SQUAD in the drama at certain times.)

This program may be presented, as it premiered in 1994 at Falls Baptist Church, in two parts. Part I features a package of Christmas Music performed by choirs and orchestra. Part II features the drama with appropriate choir music inserted. See the Production Notes at the end of this script for further music suggestions.

Part I: Christmas Music

(This part includes a short introductory reading to set the tone of the program)

MUSIC: MENS'S GROUP sings a capella first verse of "The First Noel" up to the chorus

(They continue humming chorus and melody in the background until narrators are finished)

(NARRATORS enter)

NARRATOR 1: Love is the heart of the Christmas season.

NARRATOR 2: The time when we show others our love in the things we do, the songs we sing, and the gifts we give.

NARRATOR 3: A reflection of the love of God.

NARRATOR 2: God was the first and greatest one to show love at Christmas.

NARRATOR 1: Consider these words from the Gospel of John, chapter three, verse sixteen,

ALL: "For God so loved the world . . .

NARRATOR 2: . . . that He gave His only begotten son . . .

NARRATOR 1: . . . that whosoever believeth in Him should not perish. . .

NARRATOR 3: . . .but have everlasting life."

NARRATOR 2: The original Christmas love.

NARRATOR 1: God loves us.

NARRATOR 3: He sent His Son to be our Savior.

NARRATOR 2: Sacrificing Jesus Christ for others.

ALL: For us.

NARRATOR 3: The greatest giving.

NARRATOR 1: The greatest gift.

ALL: THE GREATEST LOVE!

(NARRATORS exit)

MUSIC: MEN'S GROUP finishes singing "The First Noel" *(Picking up with the chorus and then singing the last verse.)*

MUSIC: CHOIR PACKAGE *(A package of Christmas carols not used in the drama. Our pastor wanted a lot of Christmas music in the program.)*

ANNOUNCEMENTS

OFFERTORY: Some sort of Instrumental arrangement of Christmas music.

Part II: The Drama
"THE GREATEST LOVE"

SCENE ONE: THE BARRACKS

MUSIC: CHOIR sings the opening, Christmas verses of "The Greatest Love"

CHOIR:
>The greatest love the world would know
>Was born in Bethl 'em long ago,
>The love of God to man below
>Cradled within a manger!
>Out of the East, the Wisemen bold,
>Brought to Him incense, myrrh, and gold;
>On bended knee, they did behold
>God's gift to man, the Savior.
>Chorus:
>The Greatest Love,
>The Greatest Love,
>Sent down to man from God above,
>Upon the cross Christ shed His blood;
>That we may live forever.

SOLO: He heal'd the lame in Galilee,
Made deaf to hear, the blind to see;

But best of all, Christ died for me,
O, what a wondrous Savior!

Chorus:
Choir: The greatest love,
O praise His name!
He took my place of sin and shame;
His grace to men I will proclaim,
O, what a loving Savior!

Alternate or additional verse
Choir: God loved the world, He sent His Son,
To bear the sins of everyone,
Who by faith in Him would come,
Seeking their souls' salvation.

(NARRATOR 1 as YOUNG WILCOX enters. He holds a small, tattered notebook. He is Anthony Wilcox, Jr. or Anthony Wilcox, III, son, grandson, or great-grandson, depending on the age of the actor, of Anthony Wilcox, Sr., the author of the journal in the notebook the narrator holds—adjust the name of the narrator and his references to his father/grandfather/great-grandfather accordingly. Adjust the time frame to fit however many years it's been since December 1944. WILCOX takes his seat and bows his head, motionless for the time being. NARRATOR 1 addresses the audience.)*

NARRATOR 1: *(Slowly, dramatically)* My name is Anthony Wilcox, Jr. Most people remember my father, Anthony Wilcox, Sr., as a high school history teacher, a community college professor, or as a Sunday school teacher and deacon in our local church. He's gone now, but if you could've seen him as he was over seventy years ago, you might be surprised, for he was a paratrooper once, young and tough and full of fighting spirit.

Our country's memory is fading of those days when it fought against Hitler. One by one, veterans, like my father, passed from the scene. He left us this to remember it by. *(shows notebook)* Over _____ *(however many)* years ago, my father wrote in this notebook, a journal of days as a squad leader in the 101st Airborne Division, and the experience that transformed his life and the lives of his closest friends forever.

(He opens the notebook and reads to himself, then looks up and into the distance, lost in thought for a moment.)

MUSIC: Military Drum Beats (these could be live or pre-recorded and played over the sound system. See the Production Notes to this drama for images of the music score for the drum beats.)

NARRATOR 1: *(continuing narration)* It is December 1944. In June, Allied Forces had landed in France and pushed the German forces almost back to the Rhine. The high command now hopes the war might end soon. As Christmas 1944 approaches, many servicemen, like my father, turn their thoughts toward home. He writes about it in this journal.

(He opens the notebook and begins to read aloud. As he reads, WILCOX comes to life, reading out loud in unison with NARRATOR 1 and writing in a similar notebook. After a few moments of overlap, NARRATOR 1 fades out and exits, leaving WILCOX to finish reading alone.)

MUSIC: Out

NARRATOR 1: This journal belongs to Sergeant Anthony Wilcox, 506th Parachute Infantry Regiment . . .

Wilcox: *(Writing in a diary, reading aloud as he writes, overlapping NARRATOR 1)*

. . . 506th Parachute Infantry Regiment.

(Pause)

December 1, 1944. Mourleon-le-Grande, France.

Dear Mom and Dad,

Thanks for the early Christmas present. I've really missed having a journal since the one I lost after Normandy. I'll keep writing you letters like usual, but I'll use this journal to record things I know the censors won't let through the mail. Maybe I'll share them with you or just save them for a day when faded memories need reviving.

They say we'll be in these dingy old French army barracks for a while to rest and refit, maybe until the good fighting weather comes in the spring. We got chewed up in Holland, and it'll be a while before we're back to full strength. We're out of danger now, and the hope of celebrating a Merry Christmas away from the battle zone has our spirits up.

MUSIC: Choir sings "God Rest Ye Merry, Gentlemen"

(BURNANSKI and COOPER enter and are seated with heads bowed.)

Wilcox: *(Writing in journal)* December 3rd. Today we've had more drills, calisthenics, and another five-mile run. They're trying to push us hard to keep us on a fighting edge, but after the combat we've seen, this jump school kind of stuff is a picnic. To keep us busy, they're getting up two football teams to play in a game before the whole division on Christmas Day.

Reynolds, our platoon Sergeant, came in saying we're receiving some replacements soon.

(REYNOLDS raises his head and enters the scene, WILCOX shifts from journal to actual scene.)

REYNOLDS: How's my old squad doin'?

WILCOX: If you call three guys a squad. You, Cooper, and I are all that's left of the original bunch from Camp Toccoa.

REYNOLDS: Well, replacements will trickle in any time now, and *(lowers his voice because Burnanski is on the far side of the room)* you got Burnanski this morning.

WILCOX: *(Not overjoyed, lowering his voice)* Yeah, Burnanski. MPs brought him in. Made me sign for him.

REYNOLDS: Straight from the stockade.

WILCOX: He really did what they say?

REYNOLDS: One man army. But the war isn't being won in bar fights. Guys he messed up were G.I.s from the 82nd, not the Krauts.

WILCOX: Now that he's busted, seems moodier than ever.

REYNOLDS: 'Ski took it hard when Ed Gluszcak died.

WILCOX: Those two were so close.

REYNOLDS: He giving you trouble?

WILCOX: Nah, he's been lying around, staring at the wall, chain-smoking all morning. I wonder if the Lieutenant's noticed it.

(As WILCOX speaks, the LIEUTENANT enters and stands by his stool)

COOPER: *(Comes to life, looks up suddenly, stands, and shouts)* Ten-hut!

(EVERYONE else stands at attention, except BURNANSKI.)

COOPER: *(Quick harsh whisper)* 'Ski! Straighten up!

REYNOLDS: We're off the line, Burnanski. Military courtesy's back in force.

(BURNANSKI comes sullenly to attention)

LIEUTENANT: At ease. Burnanski, I want to talk with you. Outside.

(OTHER SOLDIERS bow their heads out of the scene)

LIEUTENANT: Burnanski, I know you've heard some of this already from the Major, but I want you to know where you stand with me, as well. From your record, I see you've been a troublemaker from the beginning of your Airborne career. Even before you came into the Army, so I've heard. But in combat, you've been one of the best in this regiment, maybe the whole division, or used to be.

We both know some brass wanted to do more than bust you back to private. They wanted to throw you to the wolves in a formal court-martial, leave your hide moldering in a cell 'til doomsday. However, the Colonel let the Major and the Captain stick their necks out for you one last time. You're out of the stockade and in my platoon and this squad.

It's your last chance: Shape up now for the good of this squad and yourself. We've been through a lifetime of fightin' in Normandy and Holland. There's much more ahead because we're Airborne. We've lost too many good men. Nothing will ever bring 'em back. Ed Gluszcak was one of the best, but we have to put his death behind us.

We must rebuild this platoon and make it effective again. We need the help of every "old-timer" to get it done. We owe it to the men we've lost to keep going. Gluszcak would tell you the same if he were here.

BURNANSKI: I'll do my job, sir, but I'm not babysittin' puppies.

LIEUTENANT: You've hazed and abused replacements in the past. Driven 'em into the dirt. I won't let you do that in my platoon. We need 'em too much. You've had your opportunity blowing off steam. Heaven knows, two guys from that bar fight are still in the hospital thanks to you. Save it for the Krauts. From now on, lay off the new men and help 'em over the hump 'til they're part of the team.

BURNANSKI: If they do their job, I'll leave 'em alone. *(with a hint of irritation)* Is that all, sir?

LIEUTENANT: *(coolly)* A warning, Burnanski. Lay off. *(Pauses a moment, looking Burnanski in the eye)* Dismissed.

(They salute. LIEUTENANT exits. BURNANSKI sits down and bows his head.)

MUSIC: Piano plays "The Greatest Love" softly in the background

NARRATOR 2: Even as the battles of World War II rage around the globe, another desperate battle is being waged —The unseen battle for men's souls.

NARRATOR 3: The soldiers in this battle are never publicly decorated for heroism or devotion to duty.

NARRATOR 1: Their victories never make the headlines, but their efforts have eternal results.

NARRATOR 2: They are born-again believers in the armed forces, soldiers of their country, and soldiers of the King of Kings, men and women in uniform carrying out the Great Commission even while fighting to defeat the Axis.

NARRATOR 3: Bringing the light of the Gospel wherever they serve their country.

MUSIC: Out

(While NARRATOR 1 finishes speaking, SGT. REYNOLDS and ANDERSON enter)

REYNOLDS: Gentlemen, a new man for your squad. Meet Private Joe Anderson.

(WILCOX, COOPER, and BURNANSKI raise heads)

REYNOLDS: Anderson, welcome to your new home, 1st squad, second platoon. Meet Sergeant Wilcox—he's your squad leader—and this is his assistant, Corporal Cooper, and this is Burnanski. *(COOPER removes his toothpick and nods; BURNANSKI coldly stares)* Take him under your wing, guys, and show him around.

WILCOX: Right, Sarge.

(REYNOLDS and BURNANSKI are seated and bow heads)

WILCOX: Wilcox, Anthony P. *(extends his hand)*

ANDERSON: Anderson, Joseph W.

WILCOX: This is Cooper, Walter L. Everyone calls him "Coop."

COOPER: *(Casual wave)* Welcome aboard, kid.

WILCOX: Where you from?

ANDERSON: Glen Ellyn, Illinois, a small town outside of Chicago.

WILCOX: I'm from Manheim, P-A. *(laughs)* It's a small town outside of nowhere. Coop's from Brooklyn.

COOPER: It's a big town inside of everywhere.

(ANDERSON sets down some imaginary gear)

ANDERSON: It's good to have a home at last. Being a replacement is full of uncertainty.

WILCOX: Guess so. It's lots worse for guys going in as regular infantry replacements.

COOPER: Get herded around like cattle. Sent to the front line, get killed, and nobody even knows their names.

WILCOX: We'll get to know you a bit before we see any fighting. We're supposed to be here for a while, at least until after Christmas.

ANDERSON: Sounds good. Building teamwork takes time.

COOPER: Sounds like an educated person's answer. Ya got any edy-cation?

ANDERSON: A year of college before I joined up.

COOPER: *(mock seriousness)* I'm an educated man myself.

WILCOX: Yeah, Graduate of the school of hard knocks. Summa Cum Lazy.

COOPER: *(Yawns and Laments with mock seriousness)* Tis true, 'tis true. 'Tis sad, but true.

WILCOX: Actually, Cooper's smarter than he looks. He's our resident sports expert. He used to work concessions at Dodgers baseball games.

COOPER: That's me, "ol' Peanuts, Popcorn, and Cracker Jack Cooper." And Wilcox here used to be surrounded by beautiful women.

WILCOX: Always makes it sound like I worked in a harem—actually, they were girls in grades seven through twelve. I taught history for a couple of years at a private girls' academy where my father is the headmaster.

What about yourself, Anderson? Pardon if we seem nosy, but there's no place like the army to meet people from all walks of life, "thrown together by the fortunes of war." It's my hobby to find out a bit about everyone I meet. Tell us a little about yourself. What were you in civilian life?

ANDERSON: I was a ministerial student.

(OPTIONAL BJU DIALOGUE:

ANDERSON: At Bob Jones College.

WILCOX: At "what" Jones College?

ANDERSON: *Bob* Jones. It's in Cleveland, Tennessee, near Knoxville.

COOPER: Bobby Jones, what a golfer! Never knew he started a school. What did you major in, nine irons?

ANDERSON: Different Bob Jones. This one's an evangelist, a friend of Billy Sunday. I was studying for the ministry someday.

Regular dialogue continues)

COOPER: *(Turned off)* Oh, brother!

WILCOX: *(laughing in unbelief)* You were a ministerial student?

COOPER: Why are you in the Army? You coulda gotten an exemption and stayed outta this mess.

ANDERSON: I prayed about it. When my number came up, I was sure God wanted me to go.

WILCOX: But the Airborne?

COOPER: It's Hazardous duty. As a ministerial student, ya coulda been a chaplain's assistant n' had a soft ride.

ANDERSON: I prayed about it. The Lord directed me here.

WILCOX: *(questioning)* Prayed about it?

COOPER: You seem to pray about a lot of things, kid.

ANDERSON: Don't be alarmed. I'm a born-again Christian. I pray about everything I can.

(Pause—WILCOX and COOPER look at ANDERSON in wonder)

COOPER: *(mildly sarcastic)* "Don't be alarmed," he says.

WILCOX: Everything?

ANDERSON: The important things, and some not-so-important—when I remember. I want God's will for my life. I've prayed about which service to join, which branch, what weapon to use, which unit to be sent to.

COOPER: *(disbelief)* And God sent you here? It ain't heaven, kid. It can be a lot like that other place.

WILCOX: *(truly marveling)* Well, brother, I've seen a lot in the short time I've been in this man's army, but you're really something different! From a candid observer's viewpoint, it'll be interesting to see how someone like you fits in.

COOPER: *(disgusted)* Yeah, interestin'.

(COOPER and ANDERSON bow heads out of the scene, WILCOX picks up his journal and reads aloud as he writes.)

WILCOX: *(Writing in journal)* December 4th. We're trying to break in some new men. I've got one in my squad. He's a little unusual. His name is Joe Anderson. He's from Illinois and was studying for the ministry at some college down in Tennessee.

Looks so much younger than the rest of us after the combat we've seen. Nice enough guy, although he seems to pray about everything *(laughs)*—he's the first person I ever saw bow his head and give thanks for SPAM—maybe he'll bring us luck.

His praying didn't get him in good with Burnanski, though. 'Ski stumbled over him in the dark on the way to the latrine—caught the kid praying by his cot in the wee hours of the morning and woke the whole squad.

(ANDERSON kneels by his stool, head bowed in prayer over his prayer list. BURNANSKI stands and stumbles.)

BURNANSKI: *(Stumbles)* Hey, what's this?! *(Discovering)* Look at this! "Sky-pilot junior's" in touch with the Old Man. Momma'd be proud of her little boy.

(Other SQUAD members are disturbed from their sleep)

COOPER: Pipe down!

WILCOX: *(Waking up)* Lay off, Burnanski, let the kid pray. We'll all need it if we go back into combat.

COOPER: *(Exasperated)* Ski, shut up and let us sleep, huh?

BURNANSKI: *(Continuing, grabs a piece of paper)* What do we have here?

ANDERSON: *(Looks up)* A prayer list.

BURNANSKI: *(mocking)* A prayer list, huh? Look at this, (reading) Mom, Susan . . .President Roosevelt . . . Gen. Eisenhower . . . hey! What's this? It's the squad! *(reads his name)* Pvt. Wendell Burnanski!

(coldly threatening) Listen, Holy Joe, I got no time for sissies and no time for God. You keep out of my way, or I'll tear you in two. *(tears the list)* Pray about that one, preacher-boy!

(BURNANSKI turns his back and bows his head out of the scene)

WILCOX: *(Pained)* Joe, do you always pray early in the morning like this?

ANDERSON: Whenever I can.

COOPER: Didn't guys give you trouble for it?

ANDERSON: Sure, I got a few boots thrown at me.

WILCOX: What did you do then?

ANDERSON: Polished their boots as I went on praying.

COOPER: *(Yawns and gets ready to go back to sleep)* I'll remember this next time my boots need polishing.

(The SQUAD bows their heads. As NARRATOR 1 continues, NARRATOR 2 and NARRATOR 3 reposition as ANDERSON'S MOM AND SISTER.)

NARRATOR 1: At a small house back in Illinois, a banner with a blue star hangs in the front window, showing that one of the household members is away serving in the Armed Forces.

MOM: Susan, did you get the mail?

SUSAN: It's right here, Mom. There's V-mail from Joe.

MOM: Open it up. See what he has to say.

MUSIC: Piano plays "The Greatest Love" in the background.

ANDERSON: *(Raising his head and speaking from his letter)*

November 10,

Dear Mom and Susan,

I'm writing a quick letter to let you know I am well and moving closer to the front.

The censors won't let us be specific, but I can tell you I'll soon be assigned to a unit. I know it will be tough fitting into a veteran combat unit, but by God's grace, I've made it through basic and jump school, so I'll trust Him to see me through this one, too.

Pray for me. I want so much to count for the Lord wherever I'm sent. Pray for the men I'll be with. I want to shine as a light and win them to the Savior. I expect to meet some pretty tough cases—the Airborne are as tough as they come—but God can work in their hearts just like He has with others in the past. Pray with me that the Gospel's power will break through into even the hardest hearts in my new unit. I want to be victorious in the spiritual battles ahead, as well as any military ones I might be in.

My love to both of you. I miss you much, and wish I could be with you for the holidays, but I have great peace knowing I'm where God wants me.

Love,

Joe

(ANDERSON pauses and lowers his head)

SUSAN: He included a Bible verse at the end: 2nd Thessalonians 3:1.

MOM: Look that one up for me, dear. I don't have my glasses handy.

SUSAN: *(Flips through imaginary Bible and then reads)* "Finally, brethren, pray for us that the word of the Lord may have free course and be glorified . . ."

MOM: Let's pray for him right now.

(They pause and bow their heads)

NARRATOR 1: Half a world away, Joe Anderson himself is praying.

ANDERSON: *(praying)*

Dear Lord,

I thank Thee for bringing me to these men. Help me learn from them and earn their trust. Grant me the wisdom to reach them with the Gospel. Help me love them even as you have loved me. They call me "Holy Joe." They mean it as a joke, but help me live up to that name. Help me to be holy so that I might be filled with Thy power. I ask for victory in the battle for these souls, especially the soul of the man named Burnanski. Help me to show him the love of Christ.

(ANDERSON slowly lowers his head and MRS. ANDERSON and SUSAN reposition as Narrators again)

MUSIC: Piano Out

MUSIC: Military drum beats

NARRATOR 1: At Christmas time, Nineteen Forty-Four. Just when the hope of Christmas is growing . . .

NARRATOR 3: When the hoped-for peace seems within reach . . .

NARRATOR 2: Adolph Hitler unleashes the Wehrmacht's hidden might in a surprise counteroffensive.

NARRATOR 1: Most Allied commanders underestimate the German strength and will to fight. In eastern Belgium's heavily forested Ardennes region, where only five enemy divisions are believed to be operating, twenty-five heavily armed and superbly equipped German divisions suddenly rip through the thin American lines.

NARRATOR 2: The German High Command waited for prolonged fog and overcast skies, neutralizing Allied air superiority.

NARRATOR 3: Nine squads of German soldiers speaking English, wearing American uniforms, and driving captured American vehicles, spread confusion behind the lines.

NARRATOR 1: Thousands of American troops—some with no combat experience—crumble, surrender en masse, or flee in dazed confusion.

NARRATOR 3: Many units are surrounded and fight the bitterest of struggles with little hope. Most survivors are marched off to Germany as prisoners of war . . .

NARRATOR 2: But S.S. troops gun down 86 captured G.I.s in a snowy field.

ALL NARRATORS: It is Hitler's last gamble . . .

NARRATOR 1: To win the war by splitting the Allies in the West.

NARRATOR 2: It becomes the greatest single land battle ever fought by American forces . . .

NARRATOR 1: Dwarfing even Desert Storm by comparison, exceeded only by Gettysburg in the total number of American casualties.

NARRATOR 2: The Germans deceptively call their operation "Wacht am Rhein"—"Watch on the Rhine."

NARRATOR 3: The official U.S. Army historians call it "The Battle of the Ardennes."

NARRATOR 1: But the common G.I.s, looking at the maps and seeing the massive westward bulge of the German advance penetrating American lines, simply call it . . .

ALL: The Battle of the Bulge.

MUSIC: Drum Beats Out

SCENE TWO: THE TRUCK

SFX: Truck noise, slowly fading as scene progresses

(WILCOX raises his head)

WILCOX: *(Writing in journal)* December 18, early morning. I hope you can make out my handwriting. I'm trying to write from the back of a truck. Something's up. Two days ago, I was with a bunch of the guys watching football practice when some brass drove up and ordered us to pack up on the double. The radio brought word of a big German attack up in Belgium.

It sure caught everyone by surprise. Both General Taylor and the assistant division commander are back in Washington, leaving number three man, Brigadier General Tony McAuliffe, our soft-spoken division artillery commander, the only one minding the store. He had us up way before dawn and loaded like cattle into 10-ton trailers—no benches and no springs! So much for Christmas in Paris!

Some of the men are trying to sleep, some sit and talk, and others roll their dice and gamble, as usual.

(ANDERSON and COOPER raise their heads)

JOE: What's that you're writing?

COOPER: It's his "war diary."

WILCOX: It's a journal I'm keeping, a record of my experiences—like riding in this extremely comfortable trailer. I was a history teacher, so it's the historian in me that brings me to do it. At least I'll have it to share with my folks if I make it through.

COOPER: Yeah, "*IF.*"

(BURNANSKI raises his head)

BURNANSKI: *(interrupting)* Any of you guys lend me twenty? I'm gonna make a comeback.

WILCOX: I'm broke.

BURNANSKI: How 'bout it, Coop?

COOPER: Still owe me from last week.

BURNANSKI: I won't bother askin' the 'sky-pilot.' Probably give me a sermon on the evils of gamblin'.

ANDERSON: Rather than merely condemn sin, I'd like to show how you can be saved from it.

BURNANSKI: Fat chance of that. Your God is outta my life as far as I'm concerned. Better pray up, kid—you'll see what Hell is like where we're goin'.

ANDERSON: I will pray, and I'll pray for you too.

Burnanski: I told you before—don't waste your prayers on me. *(Menacingly)* I hate your God! I hate you! If the Krauts don't kill you where we're goin', I just might do it myself.

(BURNANSKI sits back down with his back to the others)

COOPER: I'd keep clear of him if I were you, kid. Been real touchy.

WILCOX: *(Watching BURNANSKI go)* Sometime when he's not around, ask me why he's this way.

Anderson, I can't figure you out. You have confidence that's strange to me. Where do you get this?

COOPER: *(Suddenly interested)* I'd like to know myself.

ANDERSON: May I show you some Bible verses?

WILCOX: Go ahead. We've got nothing else to do.

COOPER: That's for sure.

(ANDERSON reaches into his pocket and pulls out a small Bible)

WILCOX: That looks like more than a New Testament. I didn't know they made Bibles that small.

ANDERSON: My mom sent a pocket edition I can take anywhere. *(Changing the subject)*

Let me ask you both a question.

WILCOX: Go ahead.

ANDERSON: If either of you guys were to die today, where would you spend Eternity?

WILCOX: Heaven, I guess.

COOPER: That's what I'm shootin' for.

ANDERSON: What do each of you base that on?

COOPER: Well, for me, I was baptized in my church when I was a baby.

WILCOX: I've tried to live a good life. Always felt God would weigh my good works against my bad, and somehow I'll come out ahead.

ANDERSON: Let me give you some things to think about. First, about baptism, do you think Hitler's going to heaven?

COOPER: Ha! That dirty little paper-hanger's gonna split Hell wide open.

ANDERSON: It's a documented fact that he was baptized as an infant.

COOPER: *(Surprised)* What?

ANDERSON: *(To WILCOX)* And about good works, is there anything you've done that's greater than the work of Christ on the cross?

WILCOX: What do you mean?

ANDERSON: Listen to Ephesians 2:8, *(reading)* "By grace ye are saved through faith, and that not of yourselves, it is the gift of God, and not of works lest any man should boast." That means salvation's a gift from God based on trusting Jesus Christ. No work I can do can match that, and no ritual can take its place. The Bible says in Romans 1:17 that "The just shall live by faith"—and that's where my confidence lies—faith in Jesus Christ and His power to save.

I was baptized as a baby just like you. I went to Sunday School, even through confirmation, but when I was sixteen, I came to realize that, although I'd been a part of these religious things, I needed to put my own faith in Jesus Christ alone. I prayed and asked Christ to be my personal Savior, believing in Him to save me from my sin. From that day to this, I've known for sure I'm on my way to heaven because it's Jesus who makes it possible, not my feeble efforts or things people did to me.

Consider this: I've been baptized; I've gone to church, I've tried to live a moral life; and I've trusted Christ as my Savior—which of these four things saves me from my sins?

(Note: This is based on the playwright's personal salvation testimony, inserted here for JOE to give.)

COOPER: Never thought about it that way before.

WILCOX: Rich food for thought—I can see why you were studying for the ministry.

(*ANDERSON and COOPER bow their heads out of the scene. WILCOX pauses, then writes in journal*)

WILCOX: Dec. 18th, late afternoon. Still in the trucks. Spent most of the day talking with young Anderson about religion. Cooper and others got involved and asked questions. He really knows his stuff. I've never met anyone before who knows the Bible like he does. He gave us all a lot of food for thought.

It's dark now. Most of us are now trying to get some sleep, but it's grown cold. I hope it doesn't get colder. None of us has any winter gear. I still only have the jumpsuit I wore in Holland. They told us to grab what we could. We're all wearing two or three pairs of socks, two pairs of pants, and whatever else we could scrape together before we left. One of the truckers said Ike's been sending all the gas and ammo he can to the front, leaving the winter coats and galoshes back in England. Wish the dear general were riding in this ice box with us right now.

(*WILCOX bows his head*)

MUSIC: MIXED QUARTET sings "In The Bleak Mid-Winter" ("What Can I Give Him?")

SCENE THREE:
THE OBSERVATION POST

SFX: DISTANT BATTLE NOISE, (general rumble of distant battle) **fading out as the scene progresses**

WILCOX: *(Writing in journal)* Dec. 19. I'm writing this from the Bois Jacques or "Jake's Woods" as the guys call it. It's a large pine forest north of the crossroads town of Bastogne in eastern Belgium.

The trucks let us out a few kilometers west of town. We passed some regular infantry hurrying out in retreat—almost like a mob, ragged and dirty. You could see defeat in their faces. Felt embarrassed to see them this way. Many had lost or thrown away their equipment. We're short on ammo, so we begged what they had—they were only too glad to give it up and be out of the fight.

We marched through town out to our positions on the north edge of these woods. We can hear a firefight in the distance—the guys from Company D are buying us time to dig in.

(SQUAD raises heads as LIEUTENANT. enters.)

LIEUTENANT: We're stringing out by squads along this ridge overlooking a road to the east. We're the company's left flank. Fox Company is about a hundred yards further north.

Reynolds, set up an O.P. down near the road. Send out two men. Lay what mines we've got and have 'em take a look around. There's a farm farther east of here, about 300 yards out. You could see it from here if it weren't for the fog. Better have 'em check that out too.

(LIEUTENANT sits and bows his head)

REYNOLDS: 1st squad, dig in near the crest of the ridge. Watch your fields of fire.

Wilcox, help Holy Joe dig an observation post down by the road. Set up that machine gun we picked up. Show him what to do.

Burnanski and Cooper, lay out a daisy chain and scout this road.

COOPER: Daisy chain? We've got only two mines.

REYNOLDS: Link 'em together anyway. Maybe we'll be lucky. Make contact with Fox Company, see if they have any extra mines, and check out the farm across the way.

By the sound of it, our boys are still holding back the Krauts over east of here, but they could pull back at any time. Everybody watch out for them coming this way. No happy trigger fingers! It might be one of ours!

(Note: A "daisy chain" was a group of land mines linked together to form a road obstacle.)

(Reynolds sits and bows his head)

WILCOX: Welcome to the war, kid. Let's see your foxhole technique.

(COOPER and BURNANSKI bow heads momentarily. ANDERSON starts to clear the leaves away from the ground and dig with his entrenching tool, a small folding shovel.)

WILCOX: No, over here, into the trees a little bit, by this big one—then we're not so obvious and still have a clear view — they should've taught you that back in infantry school.

ANDERSON: I forgot—I'm a bit jittery right now.

WILCOX: Calm down. Keep your head. This is for real. The Krauts play for keeps.

(BURNANSKI and COOPER raise heads)

BURNANSKI: Hey, Holy Joe, you should be prayin' about that foxhole before you start diggin'—maybe that'll be your grave.

ANDERSON: Thanks for the reminder.

COOPER: Move along, 'Ski. Pick on the kid later.

(BURNANSKI and COOPER sit down and bow heads)

ANDERSON: (still digging, waiting for BURNANSKI to get out of earshot) I've been waiting to ask you about Burnanski. Why's he so bitter?

WILCOX: *(digging)* It's a long story, so I'll give you the Reader's Digest version. Notice that Reynolds sent Burnanski to check out the road? He's our best trooper by far. He's tough and resourceful and doesn't get caught off guard. Was a sergeant once, over in 1st platoon, but he's been in trouble off and on. Gets in fights and loves to gamble.

He was one rough kid before he joined up, but those rough cases often hurt on the inside. From what I can tell, Burnanski hurts big inside.

(WILCOX and ANDERSON keep digging while this dialog continues, pausing when they make comments.)

ANDERSON: I believe it, with Burnanski at least.

WILCOX: Has no real family. He's pretty smart, but had to drop out of school to work in the Gary steel mills. Then the war came. Why Burnanski joined up, only he knows. It wasn't the pay or adventure. Patriotism's in it, deep down somewhere—it is with most of us—but my theory is that it's the opportunity to belong to something important, to be accepted and appreciated by others.

ANDERSON: Everybody needs that. Everybody needs friends.

WILCOX: Well, he finally found some here in the Airborne. One of them became a close buddy, a guy named Ed Gluszcak. They met in jump school and became sergeants in the same company when it formed up. Think Burnanski's strong and tough? Gluszcak was stronger and tougher, if you can believe it. Guy's called the duo "The Polish Mob." In the Normandy drop, fighting in a small, isolated group, Gluszcak and Burnanski saved each other's necks, and those of many other guys, for that matter, and accomplished many of their company's D-Day objectives.

ANDERSON: Heard it was a tough fight.

WILCOX: You heard right. Then came Holland last September. Supposed to be there for only three or four days, a week at most, on loan to the British, but Monty stuck his neck out too far. We stayed there for almost two months, keeping "Hell's Highway" open.

(Note: "Monty" is Field Marshal Sir Bernard Law Montgomery, the British commander, generally disliked by American troops for his sluggish tactics and headline-stealing public image.)

JOE: "Hell's Highway?"

WILCOX: A narrow road corridor north of Eindhoven. We fought to keep the Krauts from cutting off the 82nd and the Limeys farther up the line. We were constantly out on patrol. The Germans infiltrated back into the area, grew in strength, and gave us fits.

ANDERSON: I read newspapers about some of it when I was preparing to ship overseas.

WILCOX: Probably didn't hear the half of it. Like most of Holland, it was flat. Dikes and canals and ditches all over to drain the land.

ANDERSON: I've seen some pictures over in England, though mainly about the British forces.

WILCOX: Well, Burnanski served with Gluszcak in another battalion at the time.

ANDERSON: Heard Burnanski was up for some medal.

WILCOX: He was. So was Gluszcak. Deserved it too.

ANDERSON: Well, what did happen?

WILCOX: Krauts retook a small Dutch village—only a dozen houses, a few shops, and a small church, but villages stand out, like islands, on high ground, above all the low countryside.

ANDERSON: And they cut off that main road, right?

WILCOX: Yeah, it ran right through there. They ambushed the next supply convoy coming along. Burnanski's platoon comes running to their rescue, but the Krauts greet them with heavy mortar and machine gun fire as they approach. His platoon leader can't withdraw and leave the truckers to slaughter or capture, and he can't stay put and get his men pulverized.

ANDERSON: So he attacks, right?

WILCOX: Now you're thinking Airborne! He splits up his men, coming at the village from both ends. Sends Burnanski and a squad crawling along a ditch, attacking from the south. As they hurry into position, Gluszcak shows up with another squad and rallies some of the truckers to provide covering fire.

Burnanski's squad attacks and confuses the Krauts for a moment, but machine guns up on the church's roof turn on the charging troopers. Men are cut down short of cover. Burnanski brings his remaining men through, street by street. The platoon leader's hit, so Gluszcak takes command, fighting from the north through the streets to the church. Only Gluszcak makes it onto the roof. Seriously wounded, he crawls out and silences the gun crews with grenades at point-blank range. Burnanski joins him there. The two turn the guns on the retreating Krauts. Things seem in hand when German artillery rains down upon the village. When the barrage lifts, men find Burnanski, wounded and unconscious on the ruined roof, shielded beneath Gluszcak's dead body. Troopers clear the town, taking over 30 prisoners. The convoy moves on. Gluszcak is nominated for the Medal of Honor posthumously. Burnanski is up for the DSC.

(Note: The DSC, Distinguished Service Cross, is the Army's second-highest medal awarded for gallantry in battle.)

ANDERSON: Then what happens with Burnanski? Heard of a bar fight.

WILCOX: The press picks up the story about Gluszcak and Burnanski. First in The Stars and Stripes over here and then copied in the papers back home. At the end of November, after the two Airborne divisions are withdrawn from the line, troopers from both divisions head off on leave to the same French city. A big mistake. No one's been on leave for over two months. Everyone has a lot of steam to blow off. Fights break out all over between the rival divisions and grow into a riot.

ANDERSON: And that's where Burnanski got into big trouble?

WILCOX: Yeah, but it seems some cocky guys from the 82nd read about him in the newspapers and begin taunting him, starting with the old joke that the eagle on our division patch is "screaming for help" and mock Gluszcak and Burnanski's heroism. The drunken fools should've left Gluszcak's name out of it. Burnanski snaps and goes berserk on them with bare fists and bar furniture. M.P.s bust up the brawl. Burnanski's hauled off to the stockade, but his taunters are hauled off to the hospital.

ANDERSON: As bad as that?

WILCOX: As bad as that. Broken ribs, busted jaws, and more. Something has to be done about Burnanski, short of a formal court-martial, but kept out of the press because of the previous stories. Burnanski's quietly busted down to private, and his medal recommendation is withdrawn. Sending him elsewhere might blow the story open, so he's shuffled within the division and lands in our squad. A second chance, at least 'til things blow over.

ANDERSON: That doesn't seem to be working out.

WILCOX: Yeah, not by a long shot. But we get rushed up here, plugging the line, so all that's on hold.

Even before we left Holland, Burnanski had changed. Guys who know him say he's jumpy now whenever he hears machine gun fire, probably reminding him of that day. He's brooding on it a lot. He acts as tough as ever, but he's wounded inside. I think he's angry with himself for not saving Gluszcak. Angry with God, too, for taking his best friend. That's why a "Holy Joe" like you irritates him so much.

ANDERSON: Thinking God is his enemy makes me his enemy, too.

WILCOX: 'Fraid so. It's hard for any new man to fit in and find acceptance with the veterans. Being in a unit like this—training, drilling, facing violent death together—bonds men together like no situation in the civilian world. I guess you'd say we have a kind of love for each other, a brotherly love. We understand each other, trust each other, risk our lives for each other if it comes to that. I think that's the real strength in our Army—not superior weapons or strategy, but the ties of brotherhood between the fighting men in each squad, tank, or gun crew.

ANDERSON: Jesus said, "Greater love hath no man than this: That a man lay down his life for his friends."

WILCOX: That's what I'm talking about. We've got guys here who've gone AWOL from hospitals and stole their way back to this unit rather than be sent as replacements somewhere else with guys they don't know and trust.

New arrivals like you are outsiders, like unwanted stepbrothers. It's not your fault, but the veterans resent you for taking a departed buddy's place.

Burnanski's a hard case, as far as you're concerned. If you can prove to him your worth as a soldier, that you have the sacrificial kind of love you just quoted, then maybe he'll begin to open up and accept you.

ANDERSON: I begin to understand him a little bit, and my place in it all.

WILCOX: Keep a low profile if you can, but don't cower before Burnanski. That'd be worse than standing your ground. Strength and courage will earn his respect if anything will.

(ANDERSON thoughtfully pauses for a moment. Both men sit down and bow their heads.)

MUSIC: Military Drum Beats

NARRATOR 1: In the rugged, heavily forested Ardennes region, the few roads are the key to mobility for the German Panzer divisions with their tanks, half-tracks, and other heavy vehicles.

NARRATOR 3: Like spokes on a wheel, seven critically important roads radiate from the town of Bastogne in eastern Belgium, one of them directly west toward Antwerp, the German prime objective.

NARRATOR 2: German forces converge on Bastogne to crush the thin U.S. defenses, capture the vital roads, rush to the sea, and split the Allied Armies.

MUSIC: Out

SCENE FOUR: THE BIVOUAC

(Note: In this drama, once the soldiers arrive at Bastogne, they become more and more fatigued from the cold, lack of food and the strain of the battle until they are almost completely exhausted. The actors should show this in their bodies as well as their voices as the scenes progress.)

(WILCOX raises his head.)

WILCOX: *(Writing in journal)* December 20th. Chilled to the bone. A heavy mist today in the woods and fields. The Krauts are out there now. We hear their vehicles. Once in a while, we get a dose of their artillery, although they're not yet sure where we are in this fog. We asked the Lieutenant about rumors that the Germans had cut us off.

(LIEUTENANT stands. SQUAD members raise heads, remain seated, and listen intently.)

LIEUTENANT: I'll tell it to you straight, as much as I know. We're like the hole in a doughnut, a pocket about five miles across. Inside this pocket are the 101st and odds and ends from the 10th Armored and other units that didn't get out in time.

REYNOLDS: How do you think we're set for this fight?

LIEUTENANT: We've got plenty of big guns, even tanks and tank destroyers, but few shells and not much gas. We've got little food and ammo, but our orders are to hold at all costs. Make it through this, we'll all be famous or on our way to a German prison camp.

COOPER: Thanks for the cheerful news.

WILCOX: Now I know how Davy Crockett felt at the Alamo.

COOPER: Should have brought my 'coonskin cap.

WILCOX: Your head would be warmer.

(LIEUTENANT sits down. SQUAD bow heads)

MUSIC: Military Drum Beats

NARRATOR 1: It is the beginning of the worst European winter in almost 40 years. The suffering on the line increases.

NARRATOR 2: During the night of December 21st, six to twelve inches of snow fall, and the temperature plunges near zero. During the day, it barely rises above freezing. Short on other food, the cooks can only offer them boiled white beans and plain corn fritters to supplement their scanty K-rations. Out on the line, none of the food ever reaches them warm.

NARRATOR 3: They have only a few sleeping bags or blankets for each squad. Runners bring bed sheets and towels out from town for warmth and camouflage.

NARRATOR 2: Because of the dampness and the cold, frostbite and trench foot become a major problem.

NARRATOR 1: Not since Valley Forge have American forces suffered so much in cold weather. But at Valley Forge, they were not on the battle line. At Valley Forge, they had fires, huts, and freedom of movement.

NARRATOR 2: At Bastogne, most of the 18,000 defenders sleep in frozen holes in the ground and face the constant threat of snipers, artillery, and mortar fire.

NARRATOR 1: The men rotate in two-hour shifts at the observation post. They gather what cover they can find and try vainly to stay warm in their foxholes.

NARRATOR 3: It's too cold to sleep, and the constant shivering wears down on reserves of energy. They try passing the time with talk of home.

MUSIC: OUT

(SQUAD, except LIEUTENANT, raise their heads)

WILCOX: Never been so cold before in my life. Can barely feel my toes.

COOPER: *(Jokingly, in defiance of the cold)* You guys got you're Christmas shopping done?

WILCOX: I'm wearing it—a matching set of towels.

REYNOLDS: When it was cold back home in Cleveland, I used to beg my uncle to take me ice fishing with him on Lake Erie.

COOPER: Did he catch much ice?

REYNOLDS: Very funny. It was cold out on the lake, but never like this. At least we had an ice shanty to cut the wind and keep out the snow.

WILCOX: I'd go for an ice shanty right now.

ANDERSON: I'd just go for a fire.

COOPER: *(Playing with his imaginary mess kit)* Ya know, if you mix this lemonade powder with the snow, it makes a tolerable dessert.

WILCOX: Just what we need in this weather—lemon ice!

REYNOLDS: I know what we need. We need this weather to break.

ANDERSON: Then planes could drop us some supplies.

COOPER: And drop some stuff on those Krauts.

BURNANSKI: *(sarcastic)* Haven't you prayed about it, kid? Maybe your God isn't listening to you any more. If He cared for you, why'd He let you get into this mess? *(He turns his back on the others and bows his head.)*

WILCOX: Pardon me for asking, but Burnanski did bring up a good point: Why did God let you "get into this mess?"

ANDERSON: Think of this—God entrusted the gospel message to men, not the angels. He doesn't take us directly to heaven at the moment of salvation. He doesn't have us retreat from the world and its problems. He has us remain in the world to reach other men, wherever they are.

WILCOX: That was the failure of the monastic movement during the Middle Ages.

COOPER: (To WILCOX) Oh, no! Don't go "historical" on me now.

WILCOX: Easy, Coop. Just making a connection I hadn't seen before. I suppose Jesus was the same way in His time on earth, living among the people to reach the people.

ANDERSON: Yes. Jesus, as much as He was fully God, was fully man. As a man, He chose to live and work among ordinary men. His birth was a lowly birth. He grew up in an obscure village.

COOPER: Worked as a carpenter, didn't he?

ANDERSON: Yes, before He began His public ministry. Just like any man, He suffered fatigue, hunger, thirst, temptation— because to reach us, He became one of us. One of his titles is "Immanuel," which means "God with us." As men saw Him endure the same problems and pains of life, they also saw the power of God working in Him. By that power, He ultimately won victory, even over sin and death. His life backed up His message.

COOPER: I'd always thought of Him as being so distant and above everyone else, like He looks in stained glass windows.

WILCOX: Me too. I'd never considered what He had to live with from day to day.

ANDERSON: God wants his servants to identify with other people and show them through our lives that He is real. It would be one thing if I came in here well fed, dressed all clean and warm, and preached some message to you and then left you "in this mess." It's another for me being right here hungry, dirty, and cold in "this mess" along with you.

(The SQUAD bows their heads)

NARRATOR 1: Around Bastogne and across the Ardennes, the battles rage on. As news reaches home, the American public begins to realize the gravity of the situation. In churches, schools, factories, and homes, prayers are offered around the clock for the soldiers in the fighting.

(As NARRATOR 1 speaks, NARRATOR 2 and NARRATOR 3 take positions as MRS. ANDERSON and SUSAN.)

MUSIC: Piano plays "The Greatest Love" in the background.

NARRATOR 2: Back in Illinois, Susan Anderson stood inside the village park district's boathouse with a group of friends. They were enjoying themselves at an after-school, early holiday skating party on Lake Ellyn in the park below the high school.

NARRATOR 1: Several dozen skaters outside continued circling around the frozen surface of the lake under the streetlights as early winter twilight fell on the scene.

NARRATOR 3: Inside the boathouse, excitement about the approach of Christmas vacation in a few days tinged the happy chatter of the teenagers.

NARRATOR 1: From a radio behind the snack bar came the mingled voices of Bing Crosby and the Henderson Choir singing from a new recording of the wartime hit song "I'll be Home for Christmas."

NARRATOR 2: The radio programming transitioned from music to a commercial for a Chicagoland rug and upholstery cleaner, followed by national and international news.

NARRATOR 3: The lead news story reported the war in Europe and a German breakthrough in Belgium. Other young people continued their hubbub of happy talk, but Susan Anderson's attention focused on the broadcast.

NARRATOR 1: After arriving home, Susan sat with her mother in their living room, knitting some handmade Christmas presents. Susan kept thinking about the news bulletin she'd heard earlier. The more she thought about it, the more she worried.

NARRATOR 3: *(As SUSAN)* Joe's in that battle I heard about, I just know it.

NARRATOR 2: *(As MRS. ANDERSON)* Worrying won't help him or us either. I believe the best we can do for him is pray.

(The two women bow their heads together)

NARRATOR 2: Dear Heavenly Father, We thank You that You know exactly where Joe is right now. He may be in a desperate battle. Keep him safe and help him perform his duty. We know that he battles for men's souls as well. Work in the hearts of the soldiers he's with. Help Your gospel light to shine through

Joe. We pray especially for the man who is farthest from Your light, that Joe might lead him to it. Grant Joe Your protection, Your grace, and Your power. We ask this in Jesus' name, Amen.

NARRATOR 1: Susan Anderson stood and turned toward the window. Snow fell in the darkness outside. The flakes falling closest to the window illuminated for a moment by the light inside as they floated by.

NARRATOR 3: Seems like we'll have a cold winter this year. Wonder if it's as cold and snowy where Joe is.

MUSIC: OUT

(NARRATOR 1, MRS. ANDERSON and SUSAN bow out. WILCOX raises his head and speaks.)

WILCOX: *(Suffering from the cold and fatigue, writing in his journal)* December 22nd. We're all terribly cold. Lighting a fire draws artillery. I don't think anyone has slept more than a few minutes at a stretch. Any physical exertion brings on a sweat which freezes and makes us colder still.

Going out on patrol isn't much better. We move through a dense forest where trees and snow dampen sounds. In seconds, a guy can lose contact with the squad or even the guy next to him. When we're out in the open, we lose all sense of direction with the gray sky and the fog.

Death always waits out there. We barely know where the enemy is until we're almost on top of him. The next step could draw fire from the enemy or some trigger-happy friend. Everyone is on edge from the tension—there's no escaping it.

The Germans came probing our lines yesterday, feeling us out, looking for a place to strike. They've hammered all around the southern end of our perimeter without success. Now they may attack in this eastern sector, so Lt. Smith is leading a long-range patrol to discover what they're up to. Naturally, he picked our squad to be part of it. I shouldn't complain—anything seems better than sitting around here freezing and doing nothing.

(pauses) Mom and Dad, if I don't come back, remember that I love you.

SCENE FIVE: THE PATROL

(The SQUAD stands up. The men act out the patrol scene as much as possible, without moving from their spots, as the NARRATORS describe it.)

NARRATOR 1: Joe Anderson ducked under a low-hanging pine branch. He shivered as a clump of snow fell onto the exposed back of his neck.

NARRATOR 3: He trudged through a dark, snowy forest five paces behind Wilcox on patrol. Burnanski acted as the scout, about twenty-five paces further ahead.

NARRATOR 2: Until he proved himself, Wilcox kept Joe near veterans. Because of Burnanski's attitude and concern for Anderson's safety, Wilcox never left them alone together.

NARRATOR 1: He hoped the situation would blow over, but kept a close personal eye on it for now.

NARRATOR 2: Burnanski leads them past the farmhouse, now only heaps of stones and blackened timbers from artillery fire.

NARRATOR 3: They descend to a frozen creek bed, follow it through a pine forest for almost a mile, climb over a ridge, and arrive at another road.

NARRATOR 2: The snow-covered remains of a 6 by 6 truck lie overturned in the ditch beside the road, a relic of the hectic retreat days before.

LIEUTENANT: Snow on the road. No recent traffic.

REYNOLDS: Maybe all night. I see some buildings through this belt of trees.

LIEUTENANT: Supposed to be a saw mill out there. Our engineers were cutting lumber when the Krauts swept in. We'll check it and go. Burnanski, brush out our tracks in case somebody comes along the road.

NARRATOR 1: The patrol enters the belt of trees and crouches on the far side.

WILCOX: *(Whispers, points to other tracks)* Look. Footprints. Boots. Hobnail kind.

LIEUTENANT: *(Holds up his hand for silence)* Krauts! Listen.

REYNOLDS: *(Whispering)* They're having breakfast in that sawmill building. Smell the wood smoke.

LIEUTENANT: A couple half-tracks parked outside. Could be 20-30 men inside.

BURNANSKI: *(Peering through the falling snow and pointing to the left)* Six tanks in a laager in the field beyond the shed on the left.

(Note: <u>Laager</u> is the German term for tanks drawn up together in a protective circle.)

LIEUTENANT: This hornet's nest's way too big for us. Everybody slip back, nice and quiet.

(SQUAD members start to turn to their right and are stopped abruptly by the LIEUTENANT)

NARRATOR 2: The patrol returned through the trees to the ruined truck beside the road.

NARRATOR 3: Something approached in the distance.

LIEUTENANT: *(Holds up his hand for them to halt)* Easy now!

(Others crouch defensively, as The LIEUTENANT advances a couple of steps and crouches, listening.)

SFX: Truck Engine Noise—an armored scout car

(Joe Anderson raises his weapon to his shoulder.)

WILCOX: *(whispering)* Leave him alone. Only an armored car. We've got no bazooka, and who knows what's coming behind him.

LIEUTENANT: *(turning slightly to the others)* We'll slip across, call in artillery on this place.

SFX: Another armored car passing

LIEUTENANT: Looks like recon for an S.S. armored unit. Who knows how big the rest of the column is. They're pretty spread out so far. We have to chance it in the snow between traffic. I'll cross first with Sgt. Reynolds. He'll signal the rest of you. Follow one at a time, fan out in the brush, and be ready to cover the others.

NARRATOR 1: They begin dashing across in turn

NARRATOR 3: Spreading out in the trees and brush on the other side, covering those who remain.

NARRATOR 1: Two more armored cars pass. Cooper crosses, then my father.

NARRATOR 3: The snowfall thins out.

NARRATOR 2: Joe Anderson is next to last, then Burnanski.

BURNANSKI: *(Whispers sarcastically)* Don't forget to pray, kid.

ANDERSON:(Whispers back) I am, and I'm praying for you too.

NARRATOR 1: A low rumbling can be heard and felt.

SFX: Tank *(increasing volume)* *(German tanks had diesel engines.)*

NARRATOR 2: The rumbling grows nearer and nearer through the light snow. Reynolds signals Anderson and Burnanski, one right after the other. Joe jumps the ditch and begins to cross.

(As the NARRATORS describe, BURNANSKI falls, then pulls himself partway up, and freezes at what he sees)

NARRATOR 1: Burnanski follows on Joe's heels. He clears the ditch, but the bank crumbles, and he sprawls back out on the snowy road.

NARRATOR 2: As Burnanski pulls himself up, the snow swirls away, and a massive Panther tank lumbers up, the tank commander and driver sitting with hatches open, white clad infantrymen clinging to the outside of the hull.

NARRATOR 1: A guttural voice shouts, "Amerikaner!" Machine pistol fire sprays around Burnanski.

SFX: Schmeisser Machine Pistol *(a light, handheld automatic weapon)*

NARRATOR 1: Burnanski crouches, frozen in the road, staring at the tank.

NARRATOR 3: Hanging on the tank with one hand, firing with the other, the gunner's aim is wild. Bullets zip past Burnanski, tearing up clouds of snow.

NARRATOR 2: The tank swings its heavy turret machine gun around at Burnanski.

ANDERSON: *(Shouts)* Ski, get down!

NARRATOR 1: Joe Anderson leaps up from the side of the road, plowing into Burnanski like a tackling football player, knocking him down.

SFX: Heavy Machine Gun

NARRATOR 2: The tank's machine gun bullets churn up the snow Burnanski was crouching only a moment before.

NARRATOR 3: The riders lose sight of them in the snow kicked up by the bullets.

NARRATOR 1: Burnanski and Anderson scramble behind the ruined truck.

SFX: Rifle Fire and Ricochets

NARRATOR 2: Rifle fire from the mounted infantry strikes the frozen ground around them. Ricochets whine off the carcass of the truck.

NARRATOR 1: A sharp command from the Lieutenant across the road, and the rest of the patrol opens fire from the hidden shelter of the far woods, surprising the Germans.

SFX: Small Arms Fire (M1 rifles and Thompson Submachine guns)

NARRATOR 3: Some of the snow-smocked German infantry are hit, the rest leap from the tank's hull, crouching behind its bulk, returning fire.

ANDERSON: *(Quickly. Not scared, but very serious)* What can we do?

BURNANSKI: Not about to surrender or die. Smoke grenades. (grabbing a canister-shaped grenade hooked to his jumpsuit) Do as I do. Toss 'em onto the tank when I give the signal.

NARRATOR 1: Burnanski pulls the pin from a grenade, and Joe copies him.

BURNANSKI: Onto the deck of the tank. Run as soon as they pop- - - <u>Now!</u>

NARRATOR 1: The two men lob their grenades onto the front of the tank. One lands between the hatches, the other glances off and lands among the crouching infantry, who dive for cover.

NARRATOR 2: The two men are up and running as the grenades ignite. A dense cloud of white smoke envelopes the tank from the burning phosphorus of the grenades. With the hatches open, white hot embers from the grenade on the hull shower onto the commander and the tank's driver.

NARRATOR 3: The tank jerks and swerves sharply left into the smock-clad infantry. A scream of terror cut short. The rest scatter wildly, trying to avoid the still-moving treads.

NARRATOR 2: A crunch of twisting metal as the tank plows over the remains of the ruined truck.

NARRATOR 1: Anderson and Burnanski sprint across, dashing into the tree line as the German soldiers recover.

SFX: Small Arms Fire—Three shots

(ANDERSON is hit in his outer right thigh above the knee)

NARRATOR 3: Shots ring out. Joe stumbles and falls. He struggles to his feet again and continues up the ridge, leaving red drops in the snow. The rest of the American patrol falls back into the trees.

REYNOLDS: Keep moving! Keep moving!

NARRATOR 3: Burnanski grabs Joe by the back of his belt, giving him support, the two hobbling along like in an old-fashioned three-legged race.

NARRATOR 1: The patrol, pausing only to give covering fire, rapidly withdraws, zig-zagging up the ridge into the thick forest. Bullets clip branches and slam into tree trunks over their heads. `

NARRATOR 3: Behind them, shouts and shrill whistles rise as more German infantry arrive on the scene and begin an organized advance from the road into the forest.

NARRATOR 2: Burnanski half carries Joe as they slip and dodge up the far slope through the snowy trees. Blood streams down Anderson's right leg.

BURNANSKI: *(Concerned)* Kid, you okay?

ANDERSON: *(through clenched teeth)* I think I got a chunk of hide taken off. It hurts awful bad, but I can still use it.

NARRATOR 1: With Reynolds covering them, Burnanski pulls Anderson behind a large tree and makes a quick inspection of Joe's upper leg wound.

BURNANSKI: Bloody mess, but looks like it missed an artery. *(Ties something around the leg)* This'll have to hold you for now.

ANDERSON: *(In pain)* You do that pretty good.

BURNANSKI: *(Grinning at Joe)* Nothing like Nazi's to get the adrenaline up.

NARRATOR 2: The patrol hurries off over the ridge as a high-explosive round from the tank obliterates the tree Anderson and Burnanski had paused behind only moments before.

SFX: Large Explosion, crashing tree, falling debris

NARRATOR 3: The sounds of pursuit fade into the falling snow. The patrol slips and stumbles like drunken men over the ridge and down a stream bed for a quarter mile.

NARRATOR 1: Lt. Smith calls for a brief halt, counts heads, and listens for their pursuers.

NARRATOR 2: The patrol presses on until they enter their own lines, and the Lieutenant calls for any available artillery on the road and the saw mill.

COOPER: (*Vastly relieved*) Enough adventure for one day!

WILCOX: For a lifetime!

REYNOLDS: Cooper, fetch a stretcher. Take Anderson to the aid station.

(*COOPER and WILCOX exit. BURNANSKI kneels by ANDERSON, working on Joe's leg, sprinkling sulfa powder, and applying a field dressing.*)

MUSIC: Piano plays slowly, almost melancholy, "The Greatest Love" in the background.

BURNANSKI: Crazy kid, why'd you save my life?

ANDERSON: (*Smiles and winces from the pain in his leg*) I'd do that for any of my friends.

BURNANSKI: How can you be my friend? I've treated you like dirt. You must think that I'm such a sinner.

ANDERSON: Jesus was called "the friend of sinners." Just following His example.

BURNANSKI: I once had a friend die for me. It haunts me. Sometimes I can just scream from regret. I froze out on that road today because the whole thing came rushin' back. I don't know about Christ this way—not the way you've been talkin' about.

ANDERSON: He knows all about you—it was for you that He died on the cross.

BURNANSKI: *(Looking away)* I'm pretty rotten.

ANDERSON: We're all pretty rotten, but the blood of Jesus Christ cleanses away all sin—He paid it all for you at Calvary.

BURNANSKI: I'm not so sure about that, kid.

ANDERSON: *(grabbing his sleeve)* It's in God's word. God doesn't lie.

(SOLDIERS bow their heads)

NARRATOR 1: Cooper and my father take Joe to the aid station and return, sitting quietly for some time by their foxholes, recovering from both the shock of the patrol and the strange friendship opening between Burnanski and Anderson.

MUSIC: CHOIR sings "Lo, How A Rose E're Blooming"

(WILCOX and COOPER quietly return to their places)

MUSIC: Military Drum Beats

NARRATOR 1: Hitler's impatience rages. He pounds his fist on the map. How can this be? Outnumbered over seven to one, yet the Americans still block him at Bastogne.

NARRATOR 3: The whole momentum of his offensive slips away. He must possess those roads.

NARRATOR 2: He demands Bastogne! His cow-towing generals assure him that he will have Bastogne as a Christmas present. The pressure of renewed attacks hammer on the weakening defense.

MUSIC: Out

SCENE SIX: THE BIVOUAC

(WILCOX raises his head)

WILCOX: *(Writing in journal)* December 23rd. I wonder how much longer we'll be able to hold out. The Krauts have been pounding us and pounding us. We repelled their attacks, but our artillery ammo's almost gone again. Tempers flare, and apathy takes over. Some men refuse to move anymore—they've had all they can take. There's no change from day to day for the better, only for the worse. We're weary. We're cold. We're hungry, and we're running out of time. We keep looking for something to happen to restore our hope.

(ANDERSON enters, limping. The SQUAD lifts their heads.)

COOPER: You should be in the field hospital, kid.

ANDERSON: *(weary from the exertion of having limped so far)* We lost the field hospital. It was overrun three days ago. We're short of men, so the clerks, cooks, and walking wounded are being sent out to the line. Medics stitched me up enough to limp around, so I came back to my friends.

(Sight pause as BURNANSKI freezes a moment, frowns, and looks away.)

REYNOLDS: Burnanski and Cooper, your turn in the O.P.

COOPER: *(jokingly)* Aw, Sarge, I got a cold.

REYNOLDS: Good, <u>only</u> a cold—everybody else has pneumonia!

ANDERSON: Let me take Cooper's turn, Sarge. I've been lying around since yesterday.

REYNOLDS: Sure, kid, if you're up to it. Coop can go with Wilcox next shift.

COOP: Thanks for the break, kid.

ANDERSON: Paying you back for the ride to the aid station.

NARRATOR 1: Burnanski and Anderson move down through the trees to the outpost.

NARRATOR 3: They relieve two nearly frozen guards who shuffle gratefully back up to their foxholes.

NARRATOR 2: The two men sit together silently for a long time, watching the road as a light snow falls on them.

BURNANSKI: *(Almost embarrassed to be showing how he really feels)* This outfit's been in some tough scrapes, but this is the toughest. I don't know if we'll be able to hold out much longer. Everyone's giving up. I don't know if God is for real, as you say, but if you've ever prayed, pray now for God to bring the supply planes, so that I might know what you say is true. I'll keep watch.

(ANDERSON bows his head and begins to pray)

MUSIC: Piano plays slowly, "The Greatest Love" in the background.

ANDERSON: Dear Lord,

I thank you that you love us and care for us more than we know. You know how little we have left to fight with. We need food and ammunition. The doctors and medics have no anesthetics and are short of other supplies. The hope of many fades. But you are the mighty God who made the clouds and the wind. You are the God who answered Elijah's prayer and sent rain on Israel. O God, that the truth of the Gospel be made clear to my fellow soldiers, clear these skies so that the planes may bring us aid.

MUSIC: OUT

NARRATOR 1: Burnanski keeps watch while Joe Anderson continues to pray.

NARRATOR 3: To 'Ski's amazement, the snow stops.

(BURNANSKI *turns to Joe, pats his arm, and slowly nods*)

NARRATOR 2: It's like nothing he's ever experienced before.

NARRATOR 1: When they return from the observation post two hours later, the night grows bitterly cold. No one in the squad can sleep.

NARRATOR 3: The fog dissipates as a heavy frost begins forming on everything.

(*The men react to the cold as the narrators describe*)

NARRATOR 1: The men struggle through that frigid night. They shiver, massage their feet, and beat their arms across their chests. They strive with numb fingers to wipe the growing frost from weapons.

NARRATOR 2: Burnanski shares his foxhole with Joe, who continues to pray.

BURNANSKI: (*Very slowly, excitement building, whispering loudly*) Hey, I see a star! More stars! The sky's cleared! The sky's cleared!

(*The men stand up stiffly and gaze at the open sky in wonder.*)

ANDERSON: (*Looking up, says softly, to himself*) Praise God from whom all blessings flow!

NARRATOR 1: The sun rises that morning in a sky cold and clear.

NARRATOR 3: The frost on the trees gives the forest a surreal, fairy-tale land appearance instead of a place of death and destruction.

(The men are looking up and around)

COOPER: *(Cold, Impatient)* Where are the planes?

REYNOLDS: Keep your shirts on, boys. It'll take 'em a while to load up transports. It could be late in the day.

COOPER: This is worse than waiting for Santa Claus to come!

LIEUTENANT: *(binoculars)* I think I see some vapor trails.

REYNOLDS: *(squints, looking up)* But they're heading away off to the north.

COOPER: *(Calling out, exasperated)* Hey, what about us?!

LIEUTENANT: Those are heavy bombers. Our boys have the day shift.

WILCOX: On their way to plaster factories in some German city.

COOPER: I know some Krauts they could plaster, right over there.

BURNANSKI: *(quietly, awkwardly)* You still . . . still prayin', Joe?

ANDERSON: I am.

NARRATOR 1: An hour later, a heavy drone fills the air.

SFX: Many Propeller-driven Airplanes—Transports
(Building in volume)

NARRATOR 2: Expecting the worst, the men grab their weapons, preparing to repel an enemy assault.

NARRATOR 3: But the drone isn't from tanks attacking up the road, from the north or east; it comes from the west, from the skies.

NARRATOR 2: They stand up in their foxholes and look toward the sky. German anti-aircraft fire begins to burst overhead.

NARRATOR 1: Wave upon wave of C-47 Dakota transport planes lumber majestically into view 300 feet overhead.

SFX: Anti-aircraft fire (along with the Airplanes)

NARRATOR 2: Hundreds and hundreds of white, blue, red, and orange parachutes blossom in the sky. Cargo parcels descend on the beleaguered American forces.

NARRATOR 3: The men cheer and cheer the planes passing by.

(Men shout and cheer the planes on. BURNANSKI grabs Joe ANDERSON in a bear hug and swings him around, dancing and laughing.)

NARRATOR 1: Some planes are hit by the anti-aircraft fire and burst into flames, but the magnificent air parade continues.

NARRATOR 3: Lieutenant Smith keeps discipline. The men gather only what they can without exposing themselves to German fire.

COOPER: Santa has come!

(The men act out the process of opening the parcels)

NARRATOR 1: With stiff fingers, they open the parcels to find blankets wrapped around ammunition and medical supplies.

NARRATOR 3: Mostly artillery rounds and gasoline.

NARRATOR 2: But there are some K-rations, cans of SPAM, cans of beans, and even bars of chocolate!

COOPER: Hooray for Hershey bars!

LIEUTENANT: Sort out the ammo among yourselves. Take medical supplies back to the aid station. Artillery shells to the company headquarters to pass along. Keep the food here for now. We'll send out patrols after dark and recover some more.

NARRATOR 1: It isn't enough for more than another day or so of hard fighting, but it lifts morale for the time being.

NARRATOR 2: Before the planes leave, they perform one more vital task. As the men cheer again, fighters escorting the transports wheel from the sky, pounding exposed German positions with rockets, napalm, and high explosive.

SFX: Airplanes diving, attacking, explosions

(Men cheer again. "Hooray, hooray! Go, baby, go!" etc. As SFX fades out, the SQUAD pauses, bows heads, and sits down. WILCOX sits down to write in journal.)

WILCOX: *(Writing in journal)* December 24th. The weather has cleared. Burnanski claims it's because Anderson has been praying. I believe it too.

Heavy German attack all day. Some Christmas Eve! We withdrew to another position, shrinking our line for mutual defense. At least now we have some sporadic air support.

Somebody found a printing press back in town, so General McAuliffe sent a Christmas greeting to the troops, part of it said: "'What's merry about this?' You ask. Just this: we have stopped cold everything that's been thrown at us from the North, East, South, and West. The Germans surround us; their radios blare our doom. Their commander demanded from me "an honorable surrender to save the U.S. troops from total annihilation." He was sent the following reply: "To the German Commander: 'NUTS!' Signed: The American Commander."

After dark, German planes bombed the heart of Bastogne in retaliation for Gen. McAuliffe's defiant reply. What a contrast with the true spirit of Christmas! We do have some magnanimity on the American side of things; we hear that the General let Belgian nurses sing "Silent Night" to the German prisoners we're holding in the town jail.

MUSIC: CHOIR sings "Silent Night" (Ladies begin, singing a verse in German, as if they are the Belgian nurses mentioned above, and are joined by the men, continuing in English)

WILCOX: *(Writing)* As cold and miserable as we are, the spirit of Christmas is still alive and well in our camp. If I can't be warm and cosy at home with my family, there's no greater bunch of guys to be frozen and suffering with than this squad.

Being Christmas Eve, Sgt. Reynolds and I are going to take the O.P. tonight so the men can sleep in as a Christmas present. We even have our own squad "Christmas tree." Cooper decorated a sapling with spent cartridges and empty tin cans, topping it with a cardboard star wrapped in tin foil.

Even as this battle continues, most of us can't help thinking of the first Christmas long ago. God's message of "peace on earth, goodwill to men" still penetrates even this horrible war, as we remember those shepherds out on a cold night, like we are, keeping watch.

MUSIC: CHOIR sings "While Shepherds Watched Their Flocs By Night"

MUSIC: MILITARY DRUM BEATS

NARRATOR 1: In a spectacular maneuver, the kind not seen since the days of the American Civil War, General George Patton wheels his mighty Third Army 90 degrees to the left and blasts his way 100 miles northward toward Bastogne. No one knows if his forces can make it in time.

NARRATOR 3: The Germans fight tenaciously to block him before they are caught in a trap.

NARRATOR 2: They continue furious attacks to capture Bastogne for themselves. The air-dropped supplies at Bastogne dwindle, and hope dwindles with them.

ANDERSON: *(Praying)* Dear Lord, Send relief soon. These men have little left to fight with. Keep them safe, so that they may come to know the saving truth of the Gospel. Help me to show them the love of Christ. In eternity, it won't matter if we win this battle against the Germans if the battle for men's souls is lost. Protect them so they might trust in Thee.

I pray especially for Burnanski. Help me in demonstrating your love. Help him understand your forgiveness. Oh, God, do whatever it takes, my life if necessary, if that will bring these men to salvation.

WILCOX: *(Writing in journal)* December 25th. Merry Christmas! A chaplain came by and gave each of us a new pair of socks, courtesy of Uncle Sam.

The Germans attacked us again, mainly from the north; we stopped them, and counterattacked, driving them back, but our ammo's running out again. We've been ordered to advance back out to our original position overlooking the road. I don't like it. The Germans know that position now and how to attack it.

(WILCOX pauses, bows his head)

MUSIC: MILITARY DRUMBEATS OUT

SCENE SEVEN:
THE OBSERVATION POST

NARRATOR 1: The exhausted squad shuffles slowly through the trees in the late afternoon, back to their old foxholes.

NARRATOR 2: Tremendous effort just putting one tired foot in front of the other.

NARRATOR 3: Minds feel as numb as their bodies from the cold and the fatigue.

NARRATOR 2: Their old camp lies in shambles from enemy artillery. Makeshift roofs caved in, snow and debris filling the foxholes.

NARRATOR 3: Trees more scarred and shredded. A strange silence hangs in the air.

(ANDERSON and BURNANSKI raise their heads slowly, wearily looking around)

NARRATOR 1: Joe Anderson and Burnanski creep down to the outpost foxhole, bringing a field telephone down with them.

NARRATOR 3: Fighting his fatigue, Burnanski labors at clearing the hole.

NARRATOR 2: Joe crouches behind the large tree, leaning his spent body against its frozen trunk, looking out across the snow-covered terrain.

(Both men are incredibly weary from lack of food, warmth, and sleep.)

ANDERSON: Seems like we've been here for months.

(BURNANSKI sits and slowly speaks, weariness filling his voice.)

BURNANSKI: Some Christmas, huh? Bone tired, half-frozen, half-starved.

MUSIC: Piano slowly plays "THE GREATEST LOVE" in the background.

ANDERSON: I'm sure worn out. But when I think about how miserable I feel, I keep remembering that Jesus came on that first Christmas so that He might go to the cross and suffer more than this.

BURNANSKI: Why . . . why'd He do it?

ANDERSON: Because He loves us.

BURNANSKI: *(Almost at the point of collapse from exhaustion)* So tired. Never . . .never been so weary, not just of this war, but . . . but of feelin' so rotten inside.

ANDERSON: Jesus wants to take that from you and give you new life. There's a battle going on for your soul, like this pocket we're stuck in. You're besieged by sin and need relief.

BURNANSKI: Too . . . too tired to figure this out. I . . . I know now that God is real, but . . . but I'm still not sure about the . . .the love you say He has for me. What . . . what love can He have for a sinner like me?

ANDERSON: The Bible says, ". . . God commendeth His love for us, in that while we were yet sinners, Christ died for us." "Commendeth" means to show. God showed His love by sending Jesus to die in our place. If you could see Jesus right now, all you would have to do is look at His nail-pierced hands and see how much He loves you.

(Reaches into his pocket and pulls out his small Bible.)

I'd like you to have my Bible—I've marked a few verses for you—then you can read about it for yourself.

BURNANSKI: I . . . I couldn't take your Bible from you.

ANDERSON: I have another one with our stuff back in France, and a pocket New Testament that will get me by for now. Think of this as a Christmas present from me to you.

BURNANSKI: *(Holding the Bible carefully)* Wow. I've never . . . never had a Bible . . . of my own before.

MUSIC: OUT

NARRATOR 2: Silent minutes creep by, fatigue overshadowing each man as the evening shadows lengthen on the countryside.

NARRATOR 3: Behind them, the pale winter sun sinks behind the ridge. Everything across the road seems peaceful and still. Only a few minutes of direct sunlight remain.

(BURNANSKI falls asleep in a sitting position)

ANDERSON: What? Something's not right—There it is again! *(ANDERSON squats down and picks up an imaginary field telephone and cranks up the battery)*

NARRATOR 1: Burnanski has fallen asleep, slumped in a sitting position on the edge of the foxhole. Joe's sudden words disorient him.

BURNANSKI: Huh?

(BURNANSKI slowly passes out again.)

ANDERSON: *(on the phone)* First squad O.P. reporting. Sir, Germans beyond the farm, watching for us. I'm sure I saw the sun flash off something over there, maybe somebody's binoculars. Happened twice.

(Burnanski has passed out again. Joe drops the phone and starts shaking him.)

ANDERSON: Come on, Ski! We've got to move! This place is zeroed in. The Lieutenant says pull out on the double!

NARRATOR 2: Before they can move, the ground erupts in flame and thunder as artillery fire falls around the American position.

SFX: Artillery, *sudden and loud, fading down into background and out.*

NARRATOR 3: The squad tries to get under cover, so exhausted that they seem to move in slow motion. Burnanski sits oblivious to the artillery.

(Joe lunges at him, pushing him into the foxhole, falling on top of him.)

ANDERSON: *(Yelling)* Get down!

NARRATOR 1: The earth shakes over and over again.

NARRATOR 2: Showers of snow, frozen earth. Splinters and branches rain down from tree bursts.

NARRATOR 3: Cries come from wounded men down along the line, but nothing can be done as the shells plaster the ridge.

NARRATOR 1: Slow in responding, American artillery returns a meager counter-battery fire. The German barrage lifts in the immediate area, but continues farther north.

NARRATOR 2: Survivors rise from their foxholes, coughing and brushing away the debris. Men in the distance cry for the medic.

NARRATOR 1: Burnanski, his brain finally coming awake after the rumble and thunder, finds himself practically buried alive beneath fallen earth and snow. . . and Joe Anderson's body.

(BURNANSKI calls out from under ANDERSON)

BURNANSKI: Joe, move off me. Got to get up!

(BURNANSKI moves ANDERSON'S body aside and staggers up)

NARRATOR 1: The air is pungent with acrid smoke.

NARRATOR 2: The tree Joe leaned against took a direct hit. It's smoldering stump pulverized, the shattered trunk fallen across the road.

NARRATOR 3: Splinters and branches litter the foxhole. The body of Joe Anderson lies still.

(The horrible reality of what had happened floods over BURNANSKI)

BURNANSKI: Joe! Not you! NO! NO! NO!

(BURNANSKI shakes the limp form and feels ANDERSON'S jugular vein for a pulse. He desperately shakes the limp form.)

BURNANSKI: *(In anguish)* Why God? Why'd it have to be Joe?

(BURNANSKI straightens out ANDERSON'S body, folding JOE'S arms across his chest, pulling an imaginary blanket out of the rubble, shaking it out before pulling it over ANDERSON, and kneels beside the body.)

(WILCOX and COOPER enter running, calling as they approach)

WILCOX: *(Breathing heavily from running)* You guys okay? Reynolds sent us down to check you out.

COOPER: *(Breathing heavily from running, watching around for attacking Germans)* We've gotta clear outta here on the double.

WILCOX: *(Looking around, wary of Germans)* You know how the Krauts may fire again when they think we're digging out and treating the wounded.

(WILCOX and COOPER see what lies in the foxhole. In shock, they fall on their knees beside BURNANSKI)

BURNANSKI: *(Quietly)* Joe's gone home.

NARRATOR 1: The void of evening shrouds them as they stare into that foxhole in stunned silence, each filled with thoughts and emotions no words can express.

NARRATOR 2: In the distance, Sgt. Reynolds yells for them to move out.

(WILCOX and COOPER *slowly stand, helping* BURNANSKI *to his feet. They turn to leave.*)

NARRATOR 3: With increasing speed, they run from that scene, Burnanski looking back over his shoulder again and again.

(WILCOX, COOPER, *and* BURNANSKI *pause,* BURNANSKI *looking back behind him. They hold this pose briefly before moving to begin the next scene.*)

SCENE EIGHT:
THE NEW POSITION

MUSIC: MILITARY DRUM BEATS *(covering for the actors repositioning themselves, and on into the next scene)*

(WILCOX, COOPER, and BURNANSKI now get into position, sitting together. ANDERSON sits apart with his back to the audience, temporarily out of the scene.)

NARRATOR 1: The entire battalion moves back half a kilometer to consolidate the perimeter defense. For Burnanski, Cooper, and my father, the dark hours pass in a numbness beyond anything they have ever felt.

NARRATOR 2: The expected German attack never materializes in their sector.

MUSIC OUT

NARRATOR 3: In the middle of the night, patrols come back in, and they are finally told to stand down and get some sleep. But sleep won't come.

NARRATOR 1: Cooper and my father crawl over to Burnanski. They find him sitting alone in his foxhole with his head down, holding a lighted match and a small leather book—Joe's little Bible.

(BURNANSKI, COOPER, and WILCOX raise heads)

WILCOX: You're not going to burn Joe's Bible!

BURNANSKI: (*Agony and guilt filling his voice*) No, just trying to see the pages. I gotta talk to someone 'bout Joe. He saved my miserable life again. I musta passed out before the Krauts shelled us. He pushed me into that hole. I came out alive, but he didn't.

When we first came here, I hated Joe and all he stood for. Told him the hole he was diggin' would be his grave. Now it's come true.

COOPER: Not in the way you meant. Joe wouldn't want you to think that.

WILCOX: Blaming yourself only continues the bitterness. Joe didn't see you or anyone as a problem. He saw us all as souls in need of Christ.

BURNANSKI: He gave me his Bible before . . . (*He can't finish the sentence. He opens the little imaginary Bible and leafs through the pages at random.*) Joe marked some verses. You got a flashlight?

WILCOX: Yeah, I do. Bless the guy who sent flashlight batteries in the last drop.

(*Using G.I. flashlight which has a 90 degree bend. Peers at the tiny type on the little page.*)

Here's a verse Joe marked. It's the Gospel of John, chapter one, verse twelve. It says, "But as many as received Him, to them gave He power to become the sons of God, even to them that believe on His name."

BURNANSKI: What can I do?

COOPER: What can we all do?

WILCOX: We need to do what that verse tells us to do—what Joe wanted over and over for us to do. We need to pray, trusting in Jesus Christ as Savior.

BURNANSKI: Help me.

(The three men kneel together in prayer)

NARRATOR 1: Three weary men bow their heads together in prayer.

NARRATOR 2: They struggle with the words, but somehow pour their hearts out before God, seeking forgiveness for sin, declaring their faith in His Son.

NARRATOR 3: The battle for Bastogne is not over yet, but Joe's battle for their souls has been won.

(The three men slowly rise. WILCOX and COOPER exit. BURNANSKI sits with his back to the audience beside ANDERSON.)

MUSIC: MILITARY DRUM BEATS

NARRATOR 1: On December 26th, Lt. Col. Creighton Abrams leads a task force from the 4th Armored Division, busting through the German lines and opening the road into Bastogne. The siege is over.

NARRATOR 2: The Battle of the Bulge rages on for five more weeks of heavy fighting. The 101st, never defeated, joins in the Allied counterattack.

NARRATOR 1: The Wehrmacht pays dearly for Hitler's gamble, suffering over 200,000 casualties; losing irreplaceable tanks, trucks, and essential equipment.

NARRATOR 3: Instead of ending the war in the West, Hitler hastens his own doom five months later.

NARRATOR 1: A week after the relief of Bastogne, an army major and their pastor deliver a telegram to Mrs. Anderson in Illinois.

NARRATOR 2: The message reads in part: "The Secretary of War desires me to express his deepest regrets to inform you that Joseph W. Anderson, Private, U.S. Army, was killed in action defending his country on Twenty-five December in Belgium. Pvt. Anderson has been awarded the Purple Heart posthumously for wounds received on Twenty-three December."

NARRATOR 1: That evening, a banner with a gold star hangs in the Andersons' front window.

NARRATOR 3: Two weeks later, Joe Anderson's final v-mail letter, written before he died, reaches his home.

MUSIC: Piano plays "THE GREATEST LOVE" in the background.

(Joe stands and steps toward the front of the platform)

ANDERSON: Dear Mom and Susan,

These Christmas greetings will be a little late getting to you. Our mail service has been temporarily interrupted.

I write this from an aid station. I've been wounded, but I'll be O.K. Your prayers, no doubt, kept me safe. My leg was hurt worse that time I ran my sled into the hay rake on Uncle George's farm when I was seven.

I send you all my love. Part of me wishes I could be with you, and yet I have a tremendous desire to remain here and win this spiritual battle for the Lord.

I must get back to my squad. They need me—not just for my weapon, but how they need the Gospel even more!

You've probably have heard of our situation. The enemy has been striking us, and not just the Germans. Satan has the hearts of men under siege, but the Gospel can defeat him. If something should ever happen to me, it will be worth it all, not only if it brought us closer to an Allied victory over the Nazis, but also if it brought these men I serve with to know the greatest love of all, the love of Jesus Christ.

Love,

Joe

Philippians 1:21 "For me to live is Christ; to die is gain."

(ANDERSON exits)

NARRATOR 1: In February, after the fighting moves on, one more letter arrives at Joe Anderson's home back in the States.

(NARRATORS exit as BURNANSKI stands and turns toward the audience.)

MUSIC: "THE GREATEST LOVE" is now softly played by a different instrument, perhaps a cello or violin (We used a cello) in the background, to symbolize that the same song, same message, is now carried by another person.

BURNANSKI: Dear Mrs. Anderson,

I'm not very good at this, but I wanted to write to you. By now, you know that Joe died in the fighting at Bastogne.

I was with him when he died. We couldn't stay. We left Joe lying in his foxhole covered with a blanket. Later, we returned and stood guard as German prisoners of war carried out his remains. We learned he will be buried in a new U.S. military cemetery they're preparing over in Luxembourg. I hope to visit there on leave when this is over.

I once hated Joe and picked on him because I was mad at God, but God didn't give up on me, and Joe didn't either. I want you to know that Joe did not die in vain. He died saving my life and showing me how Jesus loved me, died for me, and paid the price for my sins. I trusted Christ as my Savior the night Joe died, and so did two other men he had been telling about Jesus.

I also want you to know that I have Joe's small Bible. He gave it to me just before he died. I will treasure it always.

I'm only a new Christian, but by God's grace, I'm living for the Lord each day and telling every G.I. I can about the love of Christ, just like Joe did.

The Lord transformed my life. Because of that, I've been promoted and am back in charge of a platoon. Best of all, some other guys from our old outfit, including Joe's former Platoon Sergeant and his former Lieutenant, have also trusted in Christ.

I know Joe was studying to be a preacher, and now I believe God is leading me to take Joe's place. If I make it through, when this war is over, somehow, with God's help, I'm going to study for the ministry too. Like Joe, I'm ready to give my life to tell others about the greatest love.

(Freeze and pause until the song introduction, then BURNANSKI exits)

MUSIC: CHOIR: "THE GREATEST LOVE"

(Burnanski's Personal Testimony)

Solo 1: Who was this Christ that took my place,
Who bore my sin and my disgrace?
The greatest love, amazing grace,
That He should be my Savior!

Solo 2: He knows my name and all my ways;
He keeps the number of my days;

How can I help but sing His praise?
O, how I love the Savior!

Chorus:

Duet: He took my place upon the tree,
Suff'ring my pain and agony,
Condemned by God instead of me,
O, what a matchless Savior!

Choir: I'll share His love with those I know;
Proclaim His grace where e'er I go,
His saving power to others show;
I'll tell the gospel story.

chorus:

Choir: The Greatest Love,
The Greatest Love,
That sent God's Son from Heav'n above,
The Greatest Price, His precious blood,
Christ shed to be my Savior!
I'll follow Him forever!

INVITATION

PRODUCTION NOTES

Here is a list of the music and some production suggestions and ideas, based on what was done at Falls Baptist Church in 1994, which may help you in your own production.

Music:

Seven Christmas songs or carols are indicated in the drama script. These are separate from the music used in a choir package in the first part of the entire program as performed by Falls Baptist in 1994. Years have gone by, and some of these pieces are no longer listed by the publishers or the companies which bought the previous publisher. They are shown here as suggestions to guide you in selecting your own music to go in the places indicated.

In the order they appear in the drama:

"The First Noel"
sung by a male group was inspired by an acapella arrangement heard on one of Dr. Tim Fisher's Sacred Music Services recordings.

"The Greatest Love"
The music to the original song "The Greatest Love" was written by Dr. David Ledgerwood, music professor at Maranatha Baptist University and our church pianist at the time. I wrote the words which appear in the script. He published the melody as the song "My Savior" (originally with Soundforth), which is now available through the Lorenz Corporation website in a collection of songs titled "Seeking For Me."

"God Rest Ye Merry, Gentlemen"
And Other Christmas music, unless noted, was from a book of John Rutter Christmas arrangements for choir and orchestra, *Joy to the World: Fifteen Carols and Hymns (The John Rutter Carols)* from Oxford University Press. You may substitute whatever music you feel might be appropriate.

"In The Bleak Mid Winter" ("What Can I Give Him?")
was sung by a mixed quartet, based an arrangement under the title "What Can I Give Him?" from The Wilds, Rosman, NC.

"Lo, How a Rose E're Blooming"
I'm not sure what arrangement we used if this was not in the John Rutter Christmas Collection.

"Silent Night"

First verse by choir ladies and sung in German as if they were the Belgian nurses mentioned in the script. The men joined in on the later verses, which were sung in English. I'm not sure what arrangement we used if this was not in the John Rutter Christmas Collection.

"While Shepherds Watched Their Flocks By Night"
Orignally we used "The Shepherds Looked Up" also by David Ledgerwood, but *SOUNDFORTH*, the original publisher, withdrew it. We suggest substituting "While Shepherds Watched Their Flocks by Night" or some other carol about the shepherds watching by night.

"The Greatest Love"
Final portion to close the program performance.

DRUM BEATS
The military drum beats were played on tympani and snare drum. I have a hand-written score on file. We actually recorded the beats and played them over the sound system so we could regulate the volume. The intended effect was inspired by the old TV series "Combat," which created a certain battlefield mood by having similar drum beats in the background. See the drum beat image below for the score:

This pattern repeats over and over where needed.

FATIGUE FACTOR

Note that in this drama, once the soldiers arrive at Bastogne, they become progressively more fatigued from the cold and the strain of the battle until they are almost completely exhausted. The actors should show this in their bodies as well as their voices.

Deaf Interpretation

The deaf need to "hear" too. If you have deaf interpreters, be sure they have enough time to become familiar with your script so they can devise "sign names" for the characters and figure out how they will interpret difficult expressions and idioms (the deaf are very literal in their thinking and don't understand abstract expressions like "pie in the sky" without explanation.) Give the interpreters copies of your music as well so that they can interpret the words to the songs being sung. Have them come to the rehearsals so that they can practice their interpreting.

At Falls Baptist we had one interpreter for the drama and our deaf choir sang in signs along with the church choir during the choir numbers. You may also wish to assign different characters to separate interpreters.

Staging:

Do whatever works best for your stage situation.

We sat the soldiers out on a platform, in front of our choir and orchestra, in this order:

(Front row, stage right to stage left) Wilcox, Anderson, Burnanski, Cooper
(Back row, stage right to left) Reynolds, Smith

Our Narrators and Deaf Interpreters were down on floor level, to the far sides of the soldiers:
See the layout below:

(Stage Right)   Choir and Orchestra   (Stage Left)

Reynolds   Smith
Wilcox Anderson, Burnanski Cooper
Deaf Interpreters   Narrators

Audience

The acting was performed in a modified Readers Theatre style. The actors stood or sat facing the audience and directed all their acting, reacting, and interacting outward to an off stage focus, using the dramatic "V" technique. The exception to this approach were parts of the scenes between Joe Anderson and Burnanski, and the final scene when Burnanski, Cooper, and Wilcox pray. These scenes between Anderson and Burnanski, such as parts of The Patrol and The Observation Post scenes, and the final scene when the three men pray, were done in a standard acting style where the focus was between the actors on stage, with the actors making physical contact and eye contact.

The narrators sat in the front pews and stepped out when they were needed to narrate. Sometimes they remained standing through a scene.

Originally we sought to get small stools for the soldiers to sit on, but settled for small, two-step wooden step-ladders, painted black. These were light in weight and less expensive than stools and achieved the same effect. It gave them a step to rest a foot on, for a more casual pose.

Our scenery was simple. Readers Theatre in its purest form does not require any scenery, but scenery can enhance the over all atmosphere and adds to the "spectacle" element in drama. Ours consisted of a large flat on the wall in the baptistery depict winter a snowy forest with tank tracks leading away through the snow (similar to the scene in the promotional artwork). Because this story takes place in a snowy forest, any kind of decorations depicting snow and evergreen trees (which are easy to find at Christmas) would be suitable.

Lights:

We rented locally six 6x9's, two PAR36 Flood lights, two dimmer packs, two towers, cables, and a small lighting control board. We also had six clip-on utility floodlights using 150 watt flood lights.

The 6x9's are a type of spot light with shutters supposedly allowing you to light an area 6x9 feet. All six of these lights were mounted with light pink gels to help with skin tone. Two of the 6x9's were used to light the narrators in the foreground. The other four were used across the actor's platform, giving area lighting in four segments—when Wilcox read from his diary or Joe Anderson prayed we could bring up a light just on that character.

Four of the clip-on floods gave us fill lighting across the stage, and two of the clip-on's had blue floods we used for the night scene.

The lighting control board we rented had a dual set of controls which allowed set-up of two scenes and cross fading for scene changes.

Sound:

We did not use sound effects in every place noted in the script. In order to simplify, because of our volunteer technical crew, we used only the major background sound effects: The truck, the distant battle noise, trucks passing, the tank, the planes over head, and the artillery attack. If you have a sharp crew and ample time to rehearse the effects, insert as many as you wish.

You can find good sound effects for sale On line, such as the BBC sound effects library. Our local public library had the CBS Audio file in a two volume set of four CD's.

Costumes:

The Narrators should wear dark, unobtrusive clothing. You can dress them in 1940's style, if you wish.

Originally our Soldiers were to wear the traditional Reader's Theatre garb (black or olive drab turtle necks and black or olive drab slacks), but someone was able to get a local Air National Guard unit to loan us helmets, olive drab fatigues and boots to make our men look something like paratroopers. We found "Screaming Eagle" shoulder patches at a local Army-Navy store, and they're available On Line.

Make-up: Some basic stage make-up may be helpful if the lights wash out the actor's features.

Props: Our weapons were imaginary. Our WILCOX had a small notebook he used for a journal, which he could slip into one of the pouch/pockets on his uniform and to prompt him if he forgot his lines.) We had a prayer list and small Bible for ANDERSON to use.

Production Schedule:

Cast your parts and start the choir rehearsals by *September*, if possible, to get them going on memorization.

Emphasize memorization of drama parts to be accomplished **as soon as possible.** Memorizing takes work, it can be a weak point if you don't stay on top of it, but it is vital to the success of the drama.

Lines must be memorized and be heard—those are the minimum requirements when working with amateur actors in a church production.

Begin dramatic rehearsals by *October.* (Begin practicing with sound effects before the dress rehearsal so that the technical crew knows the timing of the cues). The Thanksgiving holiday will disrupt the rehearsal schedule due to people being out of town and unavailable for rehearsal. Get as much done before then as possible because the last couple weeks will fly by.

· Have at least one technical rehearsal, if possible, for the benefit of lights, sound, and sound effects.

· Have a run-through rehearsal, concentrating on transitions between actors and music. Make your transitions as quick and smooth as possible.

· Have a full dress rehearsal with choir, orchestra, lights and sound (and sound effects). I often call this our first performance because most of the choir and orchestra will be seeing the full drama for the first time

Perform your program. (We had two performances. Our dress rehearsal was a Friday night, followed by performances on Saturday and Sunday Evenings. Many of our church folk came on Saturday night to leave room for visitors on Sunday evening. There was also a full dress rehearsal of the drama performed at another church the week before, helping them out because they were too small at that time for their own large scale Christmas program.)

Promotion and Use in Community Gospel Outreach:

We performed this in the Greater Milwaukee, WI area, which is predominately Catholic and Lutheran. Most of these folks will not visit a Baptist church for regular or evangelistic services, but some will come for a church holiday program. We used this program as a special outreach to veterans of all ages, male and female. We had many W.W.II veterans, (soldiers, sailors, airmen and nurses) including five from the Battle of the Bulge still living when this premiered in 1994. Contact your local VFW, American Legion, and Veteran's Hospitals to invite veterans from all eras. Encourage them to wear their organizations' uniform, hats, or insignia (which will help you also identify them as visitors.) Ask any veterans in your congregation to wear their uniforms as well.

We had special visitor's cards for the veterans which were filled out during the announcements. After our performance we recognized all the veterans present by name, having them stand up and each giving their branch of service and the war or place of service they may have served during. We had peace time veterans and those who served in the Persian Gulf Crisis, Vietnam, Korea, and W.W.II. We recognized W.W.II and Battle of the Bulge veterans last. The crowd gave them a standing ovation, and our choir and orchestra suddenly began "The Battle Hymn of the Republic," starting with the chorus, while a color guard marched down the center aisle to stand in front of the platform. It was a moving experience which brought many tears and expressions of gratitude from veterans. After the program, the veterans were invited to attend a light reception with the choir, orchestra, and actors.

We used the "Screaming Eagles" divisional patch extensively in our promotional literature. It is one of the most famous insignia in the U.S. Army and brought instant recognition from the veterans and other interested people.

SOUND EFFECTS:

Here is a list of the SFX from the script:

Truck Noise
Battle Noise (general rumble of distant battle)
Truck Engine Noise
Tank (Diesel engine noise if actual tank SFX cannot be found)
Machine Pistol (a light, hand held automatic weapon)
Heavy Machine Gun
Rifle Fire and Ricochets
Small Arms Fire (M1 rifles and Thompson Submachine guns)
Small Arms Fire—Three shots
Large Explosion, crashing tree, falling debris
Many Propeller-driven Airplanes—Transports (Building in volume)
Antiaircraft fire (along with the Airplanes)
Airplanes attacking, explosions
Artillery, sudden and loud

Background on the Actual Battle:

The Battle of the Bulge (December 1944-January 1945) was the last great German offensive in the West during World War II. Following the Normandy invasion on June 6, 1944, Allied forces swept rapidly through France but became stalled along the defenses at the German border in September.

Counterattack is an important component in German military strategy. Even in retreat they were always looking for opportunities to strike back and attack. As early as July, 1944, Hitler and the German High Command were contemplating a major counterattack to stop the Allies in the West. They carefully gathered men and material and quietly massed them in an area where the terrain was so rugged the Allies were convinced it was unsuitable for counteroffensive because of its difficult terrain and narrow communications lines. But the Germans had used the hilly and wooded Ardennes country to their advantage in a similar way in the First World War invasion of Belgium.

On December 16th, taking advantage of poor weather that grounded Allied aircraft, the Wehrmacht launched a powerful counteroffensive through the Ardennes, advancing 50 km (31 miles) into Belgium and Luxembourg. Their aims were two fold: 1) dividing the American forces from the British and 2) retaking the vital seaport of Antwerp. They planned on resupplying their forces through Antwerp, creating a stalemate, possibly collapsing the alliance between Americans and British, forcing an end the war in the West.

At first, Wehrmacht divisions caught the Allies by surprise, plowing through the thin American front. Some of the American units there were new and inexperienced. The Germans succeeded in overrunning, capturing, and destroying many units, and sent others reeling back in chaos. The German advance created a westward "bulge" in the Allied lines.

The Supreme Allied Commander, General Eisenhower, did not hesitate and threw his only available reserves, two American airborne divisions, into the battle, stemming the flood and blocking the advancing Germans. The airborne troops rushed into battle overland on trucks, rather than from the sky by parachute or glider. These special light infantry divisions were depleted in numbers and equipment from heavy fighting only a month before in Holland, but they were among the best fighting troops Eisenhower had. The aggressive mindset of the airborne units was different than other combat units. The airborne divisions were trained and experienced in fighting behind enemy lines, as they did with great success in Sicily and Normandy. Being surrounded and outnumbered did not create immediate panic.

The limited road network through the Ardennes was vital to the Wehrmacht's success, but the American airborne divisions blocked them in two key places. The German counteroffensive stalled when they encountered airborne troops in savage fighting near St. Vith (The 82nd Airborne Division and some engineer units), to the north, and the crossroads town of Bastogne (The 101st Airborne Division along with some other units, including artillery and some tanks from the 10th Armored Division) in the center. Bastogne was surrounded, but the Americans stubbornly held on. They prevented the Wehrmacht from gaining the key road network there. This gave opportunity for other American forces regrouping and pushing in on the Bulge from the north and the south.

Barely managing to avoid being cut off by a massive Allied pincer movement, the Wehrmacht divisions reluctantly withdrew to their own lines in January. The Germans suffered heavy losses, including more than 200,000 men and much heavy equipment. This led to their rapid collapse in the West over the next four months and final defeat in May, 1945.

Suggested Reading:

Band of Brothers: E Company, 2nd Battalion, 506th Parachute Infantry Regiment, 101st Airborne Division by Stephen Ambrose. **This book was the one of the primary inspirations for the drama.**

After the drama was novelized, I watched the TV mini-series based on this book. I didn't want to see it before writing my own novel and be tempted to copy the scenes and dialogue. The mini-series is well done (it won several Emmys) and sought to be faithful to the book and the recollections of the actual men, although some dramatic license was necessary. It's worth watching, but take caution because of foul soldier's language, which is part of the historical context of the actual people involved.

Citizen Soldiers, also by Stephen Ambrose, one of the most accurate and honest attempts to describe what it was like to be a common GI fighting in Northwest Europe in 1944-45.

Battle: The Story of the Bulge by John Toland. An exhaustive classic of narrative and anecdotal perspectives.

The Battle of the Bulge by the editors of Time/Life books. A volume in their W.W. II series. A good basic history of the battle with ample pictures. **Everyone taking part in this program should read or look through this at least.**

The Bitter Woods by John S.D. Eisenhower (Ike's son). Another anecdotal history of the battle with emphasis on the allied commands from the Supreme Commander down to squad leaders.

Crusade in Europe by Dwight D. Eisenhower. Ike's W.W.II memoirs. Read about his decisive leadership in the early days of the battle.

The Damned Engineers by Janice Holt Giles. A fascinating record of how a small, resourceful group of American combat engineers frustrated and stalled part of the German advance blowing bridges and hampering their progress in the Battle of the Bulge. Written by the wife of one of the engineers. The title comes from the frustrated curse made by one of the German commanders.

I was Baker Two by J.J. Kuhn. A unique personal account by a West Bend, Wis. native of his own W.W. II experience as an infantry sergeant which included being taken prisoner during the Battle of the Bulge.

Patton: Ordeal and Triumph by Lasadas Farrago, A detailed account of Gen. George Patton in World War II. One of the sources for the movie *Patton*. Tells how Patton foresaw a possible breakout on his northern flank and prepared in his thinking for the Third Army's eventual change in direction to relieve Bastogne.

Ridgeway's Paratroopers by Clay Blair. A thorough history of the U.S. paratroops from pre-war through to Allied occupation of Germany. He was commander of the 18th Airborne Corps, which included the 101st Airborne Division at the time of the battle.

Seven Roads to Hell, by Donald Burgett. An excellent first-hand account of the siege of Bastogne from a member of the 101st Airborne who was there. He was in Company D, sister company to the Band of Brothers' Company E. Company D entered the Bastogne area first and held off the approaching Germans in brutal fighting in a small Belgian town northeast of Bastogne, buying time for the rest of the division to dig in as they arrived on the scene.

*A **Soldier's** Story* by Omar Bradley. The W.W. II memoirs of General of the Army Omar Bradley, commander of U.S. Army forces in Northwest Europe during the Battle of the Bulge. It details the key decision to place American units north of the Bulge, being cut off from Bradley's oversight, under temporary British command. This move thwarted German hopes of weakening the Allies by splitting them north and south.

*A **Time for Trumpets:** The Untold Story of the Battle of the Bulge* by Charles MacDonald. Another anecdotal treatment with some information and stories found nowhere else. For example, he details how the 101st Airborne's field hospital that was overrun south of Bastogne and what happened to the nurses captured there.

Also:

Battleground, (I've seen it in public library collections and for sale on e-Bay) a major motion picture produced only a few years after the war. It is the fictional account (which glosses over some of the suffering) of a squad of the 101st during the siege of Bastogne (glider troops in this case, who were part of the division along with paratroopers). It won an Academy Award for Best Cinematography. Actors include Van Johnson, James Whitmore, Ricardo Montalban, George Murphy, and James Arness. Some actual 101st veterans played background roles. Of Battle of the Bulge movies I've seen, it's the best one. (The 1965 movie *Battle of the Bulge*, with Henry Fonda, is so highly fictionalized and inaccurate that it enraged Eisenhower when he saw it.)

The Christmas Runaway

A Drama By
Randy Pilz

"But Jonah rose up to flee unto Tarshish from the presence of the LORD . . ."
Jonah 1:3

"The Christmas Runaway"

by Randy Pilz

(Musical Suggestions Included. Full listing in the Production Notes)

This story appears in an expanded form in the novella *David Youngman: Runaway Missionary* by Randy Pilz available at Amazon.com.

Characters:
(In Order of Appearance)

NARRATOR 1
NARRATOR 2
NARRATOR 3
(Who combine at times to form a NARRATOR CHORUS. It is suggested that these Narrators be female to counterbalance the number of male characters in the drama.)

DAVID YOUNGMAN, a troubled university student
SIMON WILSON, a fellow university student
ROBERT THACKER, a fellow university student
NANCY TRENT, an attractive, devout young woman who
        exchanges letters with DAVID
MARCUS TRENT, DAVID'S boyhood friend, NANCY'S elder
        brother
A FRIENDLY NEW ENGLAND SAILOR, seated before the
        hearth
CAPT. EDWARD HASSELTINE, owner and captain of the
        American merchant ship *Pocassett,* a swift blockade runner
        headed to France
AUNT ABIGAIL CLAIBORNE, DAVID'S widowed aunt
PASTOR BARNABAS NEWMAN, a kindly professor of
        languages at DAVID'S university and pastor of a small
        country church near by.
MISSIONARY DAVID YOUNGMAN, SR., DAVID'S father
MRS. BETSY YOUNGMAN, DAVID'S mother
YOUNG DAVY, DAVID as a seven year-old boy

CAPT. RICHARD FORESTER, commander of the British frigate
H.M.S. Leviathan, on station off lower New England
LT. THOMAS STURNDALE, first officer of the *Leviathan*
GEORGE, a British sailor
HARRY, a British sailor

MUSIC and SOUND EFFECTS

Places for suggested Music and Sound Effects (SFX) are indicated in the script in **Bold** and *Italics*. A complete listing of suggested Music and Sound Effects is in the Production Notes to this drama.

Author's Notes:

"The Christmas Runaway" is a work of fiction based on themes from the Old Testament Book of Jonah. It is not "if you run away from God, He'll get you," but rather the story of a rebellious young man learning that God loves all men and is "not willing that any should perish." The story borrows many elements from Jonah but is not intended to be a complete, parallel retelling of that story.

The modern, "politically correct" title for the aboriginal people of the territory which became the United States is Native American. But, for hundreds of years, the commonly used name was <u>Indian</u>. That is the name used in this script, based on history and the 1811 setting of this story, and is not used with any intended or implied prejudice.

If you produce this drama in your church or school, please notify the author and let him know how things went. You may e-mail him at pilz.author@gmail.com.

DEDICATION
To my former pastor Robert C. Newman.

Robert Newman pastored Faith Baptist Church in Winfield, IL, in the 1970s. It was the first Bible-believing, Gospel-preaching church that my mother, sister, and I began regularly attending after receiving Jesus Christ as our Personal Savior. The church slogan at that time was "The Church You've Been Looking For," and indeed, it was for us.

Pastor Newman was a man called of God with an obvious Spiritual gift for shepherding God's people. Under his preaching and instruction, we each followed the Lord in believer's baptism and became members of that growing church. Within a year or two, Pastor Newman also led my brother Ron to salvation during a visit to the Newmans' home.

Pastor Newman was also a keen student of history, particularly that of Baptists in America, and authored a book, Baptists and the American Tradition, during our nation's bicentennial year. He would have appreciated and understood the drama's historical setting. The last name of the character, PASTOR BARNABAS NEWMAN, in this drama was chosen in his honor. That character reflects, in part, the caring, pastoral spirit of the real Pastor Newman.

PROLOGUE
Scene: The Brig of a British Man o' War
Off the New England Coast
December, 1811

PART ONE: THE CALL
Scene: Brown University
Providence, Rhode Island
Earlier That Autumn

PART TWO: THE STRUGGLE
Scene One: A Harborside Tavern
Newport, Rhode Island
Mid-December

Scene Two: Aunt Abigail's House
Portsmouth, Rhode Island
Christmas Eve

PART THREE: THE FLIGHT
Scene One: Trent Farm Outside Newport
Early Christmas Day

Scene Two: Aboard the Merchant Ship *Pocassett*
Christmas Day

Scene Three: On Board *H.M.S. Leviathan*
Christmas Week

EPILOGUE
Scene: Off Martha's Vineyard
Late December

THE DRAMA

(Opening positions for modified Readers Theatre: The NARRATORS are off to one side. SIMON, DAVID, and ROBERT stand center stage with heads bowed. SIMON and DAVID face the audience. ROBERT'S back is turned.)

PROLOGUE
Scene: The Brig of a British Man o' War
at sea off the New England Coast
Late December, 1811

MUSIC: Choir sings "As With Gladness, Men Of Old" (Complete list of suggested music is in the Production Notes.)

SFX: Creaking of a wooden ship, continuing under narration. Fading out at the end.

(The NARRATORS begin slowly, deliberately, dramatically, letting the sound effects be heard along with each word and between each sentence.)

NARRATOR 1: The creaking of a ship riding the waves. For some men, it's like joyful music sung in harmony with the wind and the sea.

NARRATOR 2: But for one young man, it's like a monotonous dirge. Like the repeated groaning of a thing that won't die—the discord of remorseful memories that keep coming back—haunting and tormenting his mind.

NARRATOR 3: Deep within the bowels of a British man o' war,

bound in irons, this young man crouches in a dank hold. He ponders with regret the path his life has taken. A particular Scripture passage comes to his mind, reminding him of the choices he's made.

(The NARRATOR CHORUS is all three NARRATORS combined, speaking in unison. NARRATOR 1 gives a cue for unison speaking by taking an audible breath, a signal the other NARRATORS can hear to help with timing. Their lines are broken up into separate phrases with a slight pause of a beat between.)

NARRATOR 1: *(Audible breath cue)*

NARRATOR CHORUS:

(This is broken into sections)

"Now the word of the LORD came unto Jonah the son of Amitai, saying,

'Arise, go to Nineveh, that great city, and cry against it;

for their wickedness is come up before me.'

But Jonah rose up to flee from the presence of the Lord."

NARRATOR 1: Like Jonah, David Youngman is running away.

NARRATOR CHORUS: Away from God!

NARRATOR 3: At Christmastime, 1811, David Youngman has been running away, but now he languishes in a foul-smelling brig, thinking on the bitterness of his life.

NARRATOR 2: Some men sin by loving what God hates, but David sins by hating those God loves. His constant thoughts are about the choices leading him here.

PART ONE: THE CALL
Scene: Brown University

Providence, Rhode Island
Earlier that Autumn

(SIMON and DAVID raise their heads)

SIMON: *(Friendly)* You're new here at the university?

DAVID: That's right.

SIMON: *(Offering his hand)* Simon Wilson.

DAVID: *(Shaking hands)* David Youngman

SIMON: *(Taking a friendly interest)* What are you studying?

DAVID: History and moral philosophy.

SIMON: Will you be preparing for the ministry after graduation? Many of us are.*

DAVID: *(Uncommitted)* I don't think so. I agreed to come here for a year. I may not stay.

SIMON: A group of us prays about missionary endeavors every Friday evening. Care to join us?

DAVID: *(Cautious)* Maybe.

SIMON: *(Cheerfully)* It's nothing fancy or formal. Just some burdened students. We meet in a cow shed, actually. Not far from the university.

DAVID: Does the farmer know you're using his shed?

SIMON: Yes. We've permission as long as we're mindful of our lantern and help him milk his cows if we've stayed all night.

DAVID: So you pray through the night?

SIMON: Some only stay for an hour or two, but a few of us do greet the dawn. We're praying for Dr. Carey's work in India, for churches being started in Jamaica and the Bahamas, for foreign missions, and for missionary efforts on our own frontier among the Indians.

DAVID: *(Suddenly, as if insulted)* Did you say "Indians?"

SIMON: *(Taken aback)* Well, yes.

DAVID: *(Almost violent)* I'll have nothing to do with Indians! *(He exits as ROBERT enters, almost knocking over ROBERT in his haste.)*

SIMON: *(Calling after him)* But they need the gospel as much as any soul!

ROBERT: That new student almost knocked me over!

SIMON: I was telling him of our missionary prayer meeting. He seemed interested 'til I mentioned efforts reaching the Indians. Hot-headed fellow!

ROBERT: What's the chap's name?

SIMON: David Youngman.

ROBERT: Hmm. Heard he was here. That explains it.

SIMON: Explains what?

ROBERT: His reaction to Indians. A Pastor Youngman was trying to reach Indians beyond Lake Erie several years ago. A rival tribe raided their settlement and massacred everyone except the pastor's seven-year-old son. The boy hid for several days in a root cellar until soldiers rescued him.

SIMON: I remember hearing about that somewhere.

ROBERT: This hothead is probably that son.

SIMON: You could practically see fires of hatred flare from his eyes.

ROBERT: We must pray for him.

SIMON: Definitely! I'll place his name on our list.

(They exit)

SFX: *Creaking of a wooden ship* *fading out during narration*

NARRATOR 3: Back in the ship's hold, David rubs raw skin where leg irons chafe at his ankles while the pangs of conscience chafe at his soul. He remembers how God began working in his life.

NARRATOR 2: Many students at the university attend Sunday services at the Old Baptist Meeting House or one of the other churches in Providence, but David chances upon a small country church in a hamlet outside the city, one pastored by Dr. Barnabas Newman, his languages professor at the college.

NARRATOR 3: Before this, David experienced sporadic spiritual growth. His home pastor is aloof and formal, selected years ago for the prestige his family connections bring to the church. The reverend reads his dull sermons in dull tones.

NARRATOR 2: His messages are dry bones, offering little spiritual nourishment or doctrinal sustenance, more conducive to sleep than to Christian growth.

NARRATOR 1: Pastor Newman, on the other hand, using no written manuscript and few notes, opens his Bible and preaches directly from Scripture in a compelling, personal way.

NARRATOR 2: His messages are milk, meat, and honey for David's famished soul, softening David's heart, awakening a desire to serve God.

NARRATOR 3: An unexpected side benefit comes from this awakening. It begins during a weekend visit to Providence by David's childhood friend, Marcus Trent. Marcus recently completed his cobbler apprenticeship. He surprises David by bringing his younger sister, Nancy, along. Nancy works as a milliner. Both Marcus and Nancy now live on their grandparents' farm outside of Newport, where Marcus plies his trade.

NARRATOR 2: David has long been interested in Nancy, but none of his flirting or teasing ever succeeded in gaining the pretty young lady's attention. Now, David's spiritual revival changes their relationship.

DAVID: Nancy, I enjoyed our time together this weekend. Good of Marcus to bring you along.

NANCY: I'm so glad I came. An unexpected pleasure for me, Davy, hearing from you personally about the Lord's working in your heart. An incredible blessing to hear it.

DAVID: May I have permission to write to you?

NANCY: Yes, yes, please write! I'd love to hear more of God's leading in your life. And I shall write back and tell how He's leading in mine. And if you ever come to Newport, please call on me. Promise that you will.

DAVID: I promise.

(NANCY exits)

MARCUS: *(Privately to DAVID)* Well, well, well, Davy-boy! How'd you ever warm her heart? I thought that was a lost cause.

DAVID: I'm surprised myself. It wasn't any clever scheming on my part. I've tried guile before and failed. This time, I just told her everything the Lord has been doing in my life, and her interest suddenly came alive.

MARCUS: I'll say! She opened up like a rose coming into bloom!

DAVID: We're going to be exchanging letters, and she insisted that I call on her if I ever come over to Newport.

MARCUS: Wow! An open invitation at her own suggestion—who would've thought! Half the young men in Newport will envy you for that.

NARRATOR 2: All through the remainder of the fall term, the small boats sailing between Providence and Newport carry letters between David and Nancy, and their feelings for each other grow.

NARRATOR 1: Meanwhile, fellow students pray for David and keep up a gentle urging for him to join their missionary prayer meeting. Just before the Christmas recess, he agrees to attend the final meeting of that term.

NARRATOR 3: David arrives at the cow shed and finds the soft glow of a lantern, the sweet smell of fresh hay, and the warm greeting of the young men gathered there.

SIMON: Glad to have you finally join us, David. Brethren, let us pray.

(Possibly have several young men, perhaps from the choir, gather together on their knees in a group with ROBERT and SIMON in the front. DAVID is off to the side, facing the audience, slightly separated from the group. All are fervent and intense in their prayer.)

NARRATOR 2: The small group prays with power and conviction. Hours go by. David begins yielding in his heart and joining with the others in their spirit of concern for lost men and women at home and abroad.

NARRATOR 1: Almost dawn. David hasn't noticed the time passing as the earnest prayers continue.

ROBERT: Merciful Savior, millions of souls need to hear the good news of salvation through faith in Jesus Christ. Guide us as we pray for new missionary endeavors. Lord of the Harvest, send forth laborers into Thy harvest that souls might be saved.

(The others murmur "amen" in agreement)

NARRATOR 2: A long time since David has been with those with such a clear burden for the gospel. Their commitment to Jesus Christ reminds him of his own father and mother.

ROBERT: As you set apart Barnabas and Saul as the first missionaries, we pray that you would choose from among us those you would have become missionaries in this present day.

(Another murmur of "Amen" from the others. DAVID slowly raises his head and looks toward heaven as the NARRATOR describes his call to be a missionary.)

NARRATOR 1: As the men prayed, God began answering their prayers. David experiences something new and powerful.

NARRATOR 3: Not from emotion, nor from his own logical reasoning. Jesus' words, "Pray ye the Lord of the Harvest that He send forth laborers into His harvest," echo deep within David's soul and tug at his heart. He knows that God is now calling him to become a missionary.

(DAVID lowers his head and becomes troubled as he struggles to hold on to his hatred toward Indians.)

NARRATOR 2: As David ponders this certainty, God also begins dealing with him about the hatred he fosters in his heart.

(Pause as DAVID begins to move with a slight agitation)

ROBERT: Call one of us, Lord. Send him to the shores of Africa, distant Asia (slight pause), or even among the native tribes here in America.

(A murmur of agreement again. Pause as DAVID suddenly looks up from prayer in horror and then returns to prayer.)

ROBERT: Send him to those Indians who walk in the darkness of sin and most urgently need the good news of salvation in Christ.

(DAVID begins to become very agitated as he fights the conviction)

NARRATOR 1: David struggles. He attempts to grasp onto the love of Christ toward others without letting go of his personal hatred for the Indians who killed his parents, but he can't hold both.

NARRATOR 2: David's discomfort grows intense as he battles in his soul, afraid of where God is calling him.

DAVID: (Suddenly stands and desperately cries out above him.) No, Lord! I cannot!

SIMON: David, what's the matter?

DAVID: *(Yelling, in defiance of the unacceptable)* I will not!

ROBERT: *(He gently tries to calm DAVID and gently touches DAVID'S arm.)* Brother David, is God calling you?

DAVID: Let me go! *(DAVID jerks his arm away and flees.)*

(The men pause a moment.)

ROBERT: Let us pray for our brother, David. *(They return to prayer, pause, then exit)*

SFX: Creaking of a Ship fading out during narration

NARRATOR 2: Dampness lingers within the bowels of the ship. Mildew and bilge water mingle with the staleness of humanity, but David barely notices. His thoughts lie miles away. He mulls over the days since he ran from that prayer meeting.

NARRATOR 1: David determines not to return to the university after Christmas. No rest for him there, only a reminder of the call of God, the conviction he dreads, and others who know about it.

NARRATOR 3: Without telling anyone, he plans an escape,

running away as far as possible.

PART TWO: THE STRUGGLE

Scene One: A Harborside Tavern
Newport, Rhode Island
Mid-December

(The SAILOR is seated on one side, slightly upstage. CAPTAIN HASSELTINE is sitting on the other side, slightly upstage. Their heads are bowed until they come into the scene.)

NARRATOR CHORUS:

"But Jonah rose up to flee from the presence of the Lord,

and went down to Joppa."

NARRATOR 3: David returns to Portsmouth, Rhode Island, where he has lived for the past 12 years with his widowed Aunt Abigail, but he tells her nothing about the prayer meeting or his plans.

NARRATOR 1: Christmas is only a few days off. A fresh blanket of snow covers the island town. A festive holiday spirit uplifts the people, but it only irritates David.

MUSIC: Optional place for a festive carol or secular holiday song of the period, such as "Deck the Halls" or "The Holly and the Ivy"

NARRATOR 2: David travels down the island to Newport. He tells his aunt he's visiting his friend Marcus, but really he's heading to the harbor seeking a ship to take him away. He encounters Marcus on the way.

(DAVID enters from one side. MARCUS enters from the other.)

MARCUS: *(Happy to see him)* Davy! What are you doing here? Nancy'll be so happy to see you. We thought you were off at college!

DAVID: It's Christmas recess.

MARCUS: Your Aunt Abigail must be glad to have you home for a while. What brings you down here to Newport? Have you come calling on Nancy? You two have quite a correspondence going on. She talks about you all the time.

NARRATOR 1: In all his selfish plans to run away, David has only vague thoughts about Nancy in them.

NARRATOR 2: Pangs of conscience stab him at the thought of her and how he'll ever explain to her what he plans to do.

DAVID: Well, I'm not here looking for your sister. I'm looking for a ship. I'm going away.

MARCUS: Huh? What about the university?

DAVID: I'm going to Paris. France has great universities. I'll study history and philosophy there.

MARCUS: What about Nancy?

DAVID: I'll continue to write to her, perhaps.

MARCUS: Huh? But why leave now? It's Christmas. It's winter. There's war in Europe!

DAVID: *(Pointing to his heart)* There's war in here, Marcus. I can't explain, but I must go.

MARCUS: Does your Aunt Abigail know?

DAVID: No, not yet. I haven't thought of a way to tell her or tell

Nancy. First, I must find a ship. *(Suddenly excited as the idea comes to him)* Come with me, Marcus, and see the world!

MARCUS: I'd love to leave this dull little town and change my boring little life, but I'm no scholar, just a cobbler. How'd I survive in Paris?

DAVID: They wear shoes in France. You can be a cobbler there just like you are here.

MARCUS: I've wanted to shake off the dust of this place ever since I came here.

DAVID: You're free to leave?

MARCUS: I guess so. Nancy lives with our grandparents on their farm. I'm staying out there now for the holidays, but I've been boarding here in town.

DAVID: I'll pay for your passage, then. I've taken some of the money left to me from my uncle's legacy. There's more than enough for both of us. Come, maybe there'll be sailors in this tavern who'll know of ships sailing east.

NARRATOR 1: They enter the tavern and find a friendly sailor relaxing before the hearth.

DAVID: Excuse me, sir, but would you know of any ships headed for Europe?

SAILOR: Well, me lads, times past, a few sailed at this time o' year, though winter storms be a-brewin', but now even fewer be willin' to chance it with the British a-watchin' the Frenchman's coast. Not me, for sure.

DAVID: The blockade?

MARCUS: But we have no part in their wars.

SAILOR: England's almost alone a-struggling with Bonaparte, and the Royal Navy wants none a-trading in his ports. Few will venture it now, but I know of one captain who's run the blockade several times, he has. He's wily or a fool, but it's made him rich. Might be a-sailin' soon to France, the way his ship's all loaded down and making ready. Captain Hasseltine's his name. Sits in yon corner. Comes to business, he be a right shrewd man. Make it worth his while, he'll be a-takin' you, I'll wager.

DAVID: Thank you, I'll talk with him.

SAILOR: Be a-warnin' you lads, rumors about a British frigate off this coast right now, a-waitin' to catch Hasseltine. If you're stopped, you be a-risking impressment.

MARCUS: Impressment?

SAILOR: Not always contraband the British be after. They want men, too. Been a long fight with Napoleon. Manpower's scarce in Britain. The Royal Navy stops American ships on the high seas a-searchin' for British subjects, or those they claim to be British, forcin' them into their navy. (gestures with a tiny distance between his thumb and forefinger) They came this close to gettin' me back in '09, and I won't let 'em have a chance at me again.

DAVID: They just can't force a man.

MARCUS: It's kidnapping!

DAVID: Like slavery!

SAILOR: Aye, that it is, but when they be openin' their gun ports and a-runnin' the cannon out, 'tis a strong argument.

DAVID: *(To SAILOR)* Thank you for the information and the warning. *(To MARCUS, determined)* I'm still going away, Marcus, whatever the risk. I must go far away!

(SAILOR bows his head out of the scene. CAPTAIN HASSELTINE raises his head.)

MARCUS: I'm not so sure, Davy. You heard what he said about the blockade.

DAVID: I must go. I'll see what this Captain Hasseltine has to say. *(To the Captain)* Excuse us, Captain Hasseltine, may we speak with you for a moment, sir?

HASSELTINE: Yes, my boys, how may I help you?

DAVID: Someone said you might sail soon to France?

HASSELTINE: What gave him that idea?

DAVID: He said you've done so before.

MARCUS: And that your ship's all loaded down and making ready.

HASSELTINE: *(Looking them over, cautious)* Maybe I am, and maybe I'm not. Suppose I am about to set sail. Do you have cargo, or are you looking to go to sea yourself?

DAVID: We would book passage.

CAPT. HASSELTINE: When I sail, I usually take a few passengers, but the present European situation has made such travel, um, "unattractive" as of late.

MARCUS: You're talking of the blockade?

HASSELTINE: *(Rubbing his hands together shrewdly, this is the secret of his success)* Some risks are worth running, my young friends, if the profit's high enough. I've a fast ship and a load of rice from the Carolinas. I'll risk sailing through storms and the British navy because this cargo will bring an enormous profit mid-winter in Bordeaux. So voyage with me if you dare.

MARCUS: Rumors say a frigate might be lurking out there waiting to catch you.

HASSELTINE: Rumors! *(Laughs)* Always rumors, lads! Slight chance there's a frigate off this rocky coast in winter, but I've got fishermen and whalers watching for me. It's a slight risk.

(Getting back to business) If you come, you'll have to pay a double rate for your passage. I've no need of extra crew.

DAVID: I have this *(shows him money pouch)*.

HASSELTINE: Ah! A fat enough purse!

DAVID: When do you set sail, if you do?

HASSELTINE: *(Lowers his voice, glances around to see if anyone else is listening)* I may up anchor at dawn on Christmas Day. My ship's the Pocassett. Be at the dock with your money before sun-up on that morning if you're coming, but *(glances around)* don't tell anyone.

(Characters pause and exit during intro to song)

Scene Two: Aunt Abigail's House
Portsmouth, Rhode Island
Christmas Eve

MUSIC: "O HOLY NIGHT"

(Characters for Scene Three enter. AUNT ABIGAIL, PASTOR NEWMAN, and DAVID stand with heads bowed.)

NARRATOR 3: The fires of conviction subsided within David's soul as he planned for a life far away. Only a few embers troubled him, but they flared up again on Christmas Eve and burned hot indeed.

(PASTOR NEWMAN enters, stomping his feet and brushing off snow)

PASTOR NEWMAN: Merry Christmas, Abigail! Thank you for inviting me.

AUNT ABIGAIL: *(Greeting PASTOR NEWMAN as if he had just arrived at the door to her house.)* Merry Christmas to you, Barnabas! You're quite welcome. I'm so glad you could come! Davy, come here and help Pastor Newman with his overcoat.

NARRATOR 2: Of all the people David did <u>not</u> want to see, it was kindly old Pastor Barnabas Newman, languages professor at the university and shepherd of the country church David attended.

(DAVID raises his head.)

DAVID: *(Concerned. Lowering his voice so Pastor Newman can't hear)* Auntie, you didn't tell me Pastor Newman was coming!

AUNT ABIGAIL: *(Merrily laughing)* It's a last-minute thing. He's a dear old friend and hasn't visited here since your uncle died. He's to spend the holidays.

(AUNT ABIGAIL, PASTOR NEWMAN, and DAVID have heads bowed during narration)

NARRATOR 1: David remained quiet during dinner.

NARRATOR 3: Several other family friends joined them for the meal. David kept to himself as Pastor Newman shared the exciting news about William Carey's translation of the New Testament into the Marathi language, having read a recent dispatch from India.

NARRATOR 2: Everyone else enjoyed themselves, but miserable David sat picking at his food. At last, the meal drew to a close.

AUNT ABIGAIL: Pastor Newman, would you care for some flummery? It's an old family recipe.

PASTOR NEWMAN: Later, perhaps. I can't eat another bite presently. *(Laughs, pats his stomach)* You've stuffed me like a Christmas goose! *(Sighs, becomes serious)* I must speak a private word with young David in your husband's library, if I may.

AUNT ABIGAIL: Make yourself at home. You spent many hours in that library in days past, when you were a young pastor nearby.

PASTOR NEWMAN: Those were blessed days. I've missed your late husband and his books.

(AUNT ABIGAIL exits)

NARRATOR 3: Pastor Newman led the way into the library and closed the sliding doors.

(DAVID and PASTOR NEWMAN raise heads)

PASTOR NEWMAN: You have an outstanding heritage, David. Your grandfather and father were notable Baptist preachers. Your late uncle was a dedicated Christian layman. My privilege to know them and co-labor with them on occasion. Your grandfather, as I remember, was a great admirer of David Brainerd, the missionary to the Indians.

DAVID: *(Hot and uncomfortable)* They were classmates at Yale.

PASTOR NEWMAN: He named your father after him. And you bear your father's name as well—David Brainerd Youngman. *(Getting to the point)* Some of your school friends are asking about you.

DAVID: Who's that?

PASTOR NEWMAN: Simon Wilson and Robert Thacker, among others. You attended one of their cow shed prayer meetings this past term.

DAVID: *(Defensive, brushing it off)* It was merely an exercise in piety. I was impressed with the earnestness of those involved.

PASTOR NEWMAN: You grew agitated and ran from that meeting.

DAVID: I was uncomfortable. I had to get away.

PASTOR NEWMAN: Tell me honestly, is God calling you to serve Him in a special way?

DAVID: I— *(Opens his mouth to speak some excuse, but remains silent, and turns away.)*

MUSIC: Piano plays "Softly And Tenderly, Jesus Is Calling" in the background, beneath the dialogue

PASTOR NEWMAN: David, God has a purpose for your life. Your parents prayed for this often when you were little. They prayed you'd continue in the ministry God had given them.

DAVID: *(Taken by surprise)* I—I don't remember anything about that.

PASTOR NEWMAN: Perhaps those prayers were being answered back at the university in that student prayer meeting. Seems God has called you to bring the good news of salvation to many souls in desperate need.

DAVID: How do you know?

PASTOR NEWMAN: A deduction, a supposition on my part, perhaps. Am I correct?

DAVID: *(Evasive)* Maybe.

PASTOR NEWMAN: Permit me to deduce, to suppose, further. Let's say God's calling you where you don't want to go. Your hatred of Indians is well known. Perhaps you're unwilling to yield that hatred to the Lord.

DAVID: They killed my parents!

PASTOR NEWMAN: Yet it wasn't all Indians who killed them,

just those raiders from a particular village from a particular tribe, but your hatred runs very broad. Here it is, Christmas Eve, and you know little of the spirit of forgiveness coming from the Christ of Christmas.

DAVID: *(Defensive)* How would you feel?

PASTOR NEWMAN: How does God feel? On that first Christmas, "God so loved the world" that He sent His only begotten Son, knowing full well that the world of men He loves would reject and slay His Son. Yet, it was for all lost sinners that Jesus suffered, died, and rose again. Remember Christ's prayer from the cross, "Father, forgive them for they know not what they do?" His forgiveness even includes the men who crucified Him.

DAVID: My parents' killers were merciless brutes. I can't love them, and I don't ask God to, either.

PASTOR NEWMAN: But God is love, David. He doesn't have to make Himself love—His nature is sacrificial love. Christ loves all men and died that all might receive forgiveness from sin, offering His mercy to even merciless killers. I venture to guess He's appointed you to bear the message of that forgiveness.

DAVID: *(Angry)* You want me to forget the shouts of my father?! The screams of my mother?! I won't! (pause, feeling the pain inside) I can't!

PASTOR NEWMAN: God hasn't forgotten them either. They were slain in His service. Psalm 116 tells us, "Precious in the sight of the Lord is the death of His saints." God knows and understands your hurt, your loss, and feels it with you. Others have felt such loss, and grace from Jesus Christ has helped them through it. That grace is available for you as well.

DAVID: Sir, I really must be going. I have other things I must attend to.

MUSIC: Piano Out.

PASTOR NEWMAN: I'm almost finished, but I have a story to tell you, which is the main reason for this talk. May I?

DAVID: If you must, sir.

PASTOR NEWMAN: Bear with me. (*Pauses*) Picture in your mind a young man, a bit older than you, studying for the ministry, but that young man has a deep problem in his life. That problem is hate. He hates the French, who killed his two older brothers during the Fort Ticonderoga campaign back in 1760. The young man was only a little boy then, like you were when your parents were slain. From that time, he nurtures a growing, bitter hatred for the French.

Sixteen years later came Lexington, Concord, and Bunker Hill. The pastor the young man studies under is a ranking militia officer, and the young man is a militia lieutenant serving as his aide. The pastor joins Washington's staff, bringing the young lieutenant with him. Seeking help against the British, the Continental Congress enters into an alliance with the French. General Washington appoints that young lieutenant as an interpreter and liaison with French troops landing here in Rhode Island.

DAVID: But, as you say, he hates the French.

PASTOR NEWMAN: Oh, he does indeed! He's learned about them, learned their culture and their language well, but as a tool for revenge someday. Now he must assist them in every way possible. Torn between hatred and patriotism, the young man decides to go away, though it'll make him an outcast, no better than a Tory. He's in the very act of writing his resignation, quitting his commission, when his pastor finds him.

DAVID: And the pastor stopped him?

PASTOR NEWMAN: All the pastor can do is counsel him. Much as I'm counseling you, he urges the young lieutenant to submit his will to the Savior, yield his hate, and perform his duty to the Lord and to his country.

It's a struggle for that lieutenant, praying all night in his quarters, but by the grace of God, he does yield his heart. An enormous weight passes from him. God blesses, and good things happen in his life and in his service from that time onward.

DAVID: That was different. The French helped us win at Yorktown.

PASTOR NEWMAN: There's no way of knowing it then. Many dark days lay ahead before the Lord guides to Yorktown. I'm not saying that the final victory is due to the young lieutenant's submission and service. Still, later years of fruitful pastoral ministry do come from triumph over his hate. I should know. I was that young lieutenant.

DAVID: You struggled with hate? You're one of the kindest, most loving men I've ever met.

PASTOR NEWMAN: I can take no credit for the transformation in my life. It's all the Lord's doing. He convicted my heart, forgave my sin, and released me from my bitterness. God will transform you, too, David, if you'll surrender your will to Him. He wants your parents' ministry to bring victory, not defeat. You can be the agent of that victory.

DAVID: Me?! How could that be possible?

PASTOR NEWMAN: What happened to your parents was done in the darkness of sin. Now you have the opportunity to bring light, the Gospel light, into that darkness.

DAVID: Bring the Gospel to savage killers?!

PASTOR NEWMAN: Some in Christian circles here and abroad condemn the revival in foreign missionary work we've seen in recent years. They're appalled that men would "take the holy Gospel to the heathen." But Scripture tells us that "God is not willing that any should perish." Savage or civilized, all men are sinners needing the Savior. Proclaiming the good news of salvation is every Christian's sacred commission.

DAVID: So you say.

PASTOR NEWMAN: So our Lord Jesus Himself says, "Go ye into all the world and preach the Gospel to every creature." Who might warn those native people to escape the destruction of their souls if you disobey God's call? The Epistle to the Romans makes it clear, "How will they believe in Him of whom they have not heard, and how shall they hear without a preacher?" It's a simple truth: People must understand certain basic things about sin and about Jesus Christ to be saved. Someone must tell them.

DAVID: Someone else, perhaps—Simon or Robert, not me!

PASTOR NEWMAN: If God has called you, David, you are the one who must go. It's His will for your life. The eternal destiny of others depends on your obedience.

DAVID: What they did to me and my parents can't be merely brushed aside!

PASTOR NEWMAN: *(Drawing a folded, multi-page letter from his coat pocket, adjusting his eyes and spectacles, and reading)* Are you familiar with these words? ". . . for I am ready not to be bound only, . . . (Drops out as MISSIONARY YOUNGMAN continues the rest of the verse)*

(MISSIONARY YOUNGMAN and MRS. YOUNGMAN in a scene from the past, enter the stage off to one side. MRS. Youngman stands with head bowed, out of the scene for the moment.)

MISSIONARY YOUNGMAN: *(Coming in along with PASTOR NEWMAN and completing the verse)* "… not to be bound only, but also to die for the name of the Lord Jesus."

PASTOR NEWMAN: Do you know who wrote that?

DAVID: *(Not sure of what PASTOR NEWMAN is getting at)* The Apostle Paul, I suppose.

PASTOR NEWMAN: Those were Paul's words paraphrased by your father as he closed this long letter written to me the Christmas just before he died.

DAVID: My father's words written to you?

PASTOR NEWMAN: Yes. We began collaborating on a translation of the New Testament, which he hoped to make for the tribes he was evangelizing. There was regular correspondence between us, as I advised him. *(Handing DAVID the letter)* Take this letter. Keep it. Read it for yourself. Reread it many times. Let your father speak to you.

DAVID: *(Looking at the letter)* My father wrote this?

PASTOR NEWMAN: Yes, and from what I read there, it's almost as if he were writing it to you now as much as he was writing to me back then. You'll see he knew the dangers he faced; knew that trouble was imminent. But you'll also read there that he knew no greater cause than the glorious Gospel of his Savior, Jesus Christ. It's to this exact great cause that God is calling you.

DAVID: I'm not so sure.

PASTOR NEWMAN: You trusted Christ for your own salvation, David. You were seven years old, I believe. Your father mentions it in that letter.

(DAVID and PASTOR NEWMAN bow heads as the scene with DAVID'S parents continues in flashback)

MUSIC: Piano plays "Depth Of Mercy" by Charles Wesley (hymn tune SEYMOUR), or some other period hymn in background beneath the flashback scene.

MISSIONARY YOUNGMAN: *(Continuing to speak from his letter to PASTOR NEWMAN)* My Dear Newman,

I am writing to you with some joyful news!

As I have previously described, the work here has been difficult. Progress in the Gospel is slow, as we reach out to these tribes who have no concept of our God or His Word. So I take for my model the Apostle Paul at Mars Hill in Athens, beginning with the basics of Creation and moving on from there.

Language study has advanced dramatically since the chief granted us permission to establish this mission station closer to his villages. Now we have daily interaction with the people and learn a lot from them. Young Davy surpasses us all. Playing with Indian children has given him practical knowledge of their tongue. He learns new words all the time and teaches them to his mother and me.

As you know, I preached my way through the four gospels while learning their language. The notes I made while doing that will assist us in our translation work. Recently, I felt confident enough to begin preaching directly in their tongue, without an interpreter, and continued working through the Book of Acts. Moving away from the safety of the White settlements and these new messages on my own have created a greater interest among the people. Larger groups come to listen. Instead of ten or fifteen, I speak to twenty or thirty, sometimes more. Little spiritual response has come from this so far, but God is always good. At a time when I'd let discouragement about the lack of response creep upon me, the Lord encouraged my heart greatly in the work of the Gospel, showing me unexpected fruit.

(The YOUNGMAN FAMILY reenacts the following scene of the news of YOUNG DAVID'S salvation. MRS. YOUNGMAN raises her head.)

MRS. YOUNGMAN: Your preaching improves each time, dear. You hardly faltered today. I could follow almost everything you said.

MISSIONARY YOUNGMAN: But not much fruit so far, for all the effort.

MRS. YOUNGMAN: But they continue coming to hear you just the same.

MISSIONARY YOUNGMAN: Oh, Betsy, sometimes I wonder if I'm getting through at all or just providing some odd form of entertainment for them.

MRS. YOUNGMAN: David, you got through to one today, a little boy.

MISSIONARY YOUNGMAN: Really? Is it Abook-sigun or Mak-kapitew? Did he stay so I could talk with him?

MRS. YOUNGMAN: It's someone else, and he does want to tell you about it.

MISSIONARY YOUNGMAN: Who is it?

MRS. YOUNGMAN: Our own son, Davy!

MISSIONARY YOUNGMAN: *(Pleasantly surprised)* Davy?!

MRS. YOUNGMAN: God has worked in his heart! *(Calling)* Davy, Papa will talk with you now.

(YOUNG DAVY comes running in as MRS. YOUNGMAN steps to one

side.)

YOUNG DAVY: *(Excited and earnest)* Papa! Papa! I did what you said!

MISSIONARY YOUNGMAN: Did what?

YOUNG DAVY: I prayed to God, like you told us. I believed on the Lord Jesus just like that man in your sermon today!

MISSIONARY YOUNGMAN: The Philippian Jailer? I had trouble explaining him in their language.

YOUNG DAVY: But I heard you. You said Paul told him, "Believe on the Lord Jesus Christ, and you will be saved." That's what I did.

MISSIONARY YOUNGMAN: Asking God to save you from sin and trusting Jesus to be your Savior?

YOUNG DAVY: Yes! Like how you told the people. I prayed and did it too.

MISSIONARY YOUNGMAN: Oh, Davy! God be praised! This is wonderful news! Let us pray and give thanks!

(The YOUNGMAN FAMILY moves closer together. MISSIONARY YOUNGMAN: kneels down, putting his hand on YOUNG DAVY'S shoulder. Mrs. YOUNGMAN moves in and places a hand on the other shoulder. They bow together as if in prayer, and out of the scene.)

(Returning to the present and continuing the conversation between DAVID and PASTOR NEWMAN)

MUSIC: Piano Out

PASTOR NEWMAN: How your parents rejoiced!

DAVID: They did. I'd—I'd forgotten that.

PASTOR NEWMAN: You may have forgotten it, and you may try to run away now, but because of your salvation, the Holy Spirit is always within you. Wherever you run, because God loves you, He'll always be with you—chastening, convicting, and calling you back to Himself.

DAVID: (*Evasive*) Who said anything about running away?

PASTOR NEWMAN: The marks of it are on you. Your thoughts, your actions lie open before me because I've been in your shoes. I know your three choices: Obey this call of God, resist it in bitterness, or try fleeing from it. You're a young man of action. If you won't obey, you'll run away rather than decline in personal stagnation.

DAVID: It's impossible for me to forgive those killers for what they did to me and my parents.

PASTOR NEWMAN: Through Jesus Christ, all forgiveness is possible. Twice now, you've said, "what they did to <u>ME</u> and my parents," putting the "me" first and then your parents.

DAVID: Just a slip of grammar.

PASTOR NEWMAN: Others have suffered as well. The people your parents were reaching have faced hard times. The British have been stirring up warfare again among the tribes. Strife with encroaching settlers has also taken a toll. Those people need you. This could be a spiritual healing for both you and them. Let me mentor you in the ministry while you finish at the university and help you go out to those people.

DAVID: I'd rather go away than go to them.

PASTOR NEWMAN: There, you've honestly said it! Go away, and you'll miss the great joy the Lord desires for you in fulfilling His purpose for your life. Your parents knew that joy and desired for you to experience it too.

DAVID: *(Irritated)* Sir, are you about finished?

PASTOR NEWMAN: I wouldn't do right as a pastor without leaving you a sober warning.

DAVID: What kind of warning?

PASTOR NEWMAN: There's a Bible on the bookstand beside you. Please read from the Old Testament Book of Jonah for me.

DAVID: Why Jonah?

PASTOR NEWMAN: Consider the first chapter, verse seventeen.

DAVID: *(Turning pages in a large Bible, finds the place, reads aloud)* "Now the LORD had prepared a great fish to swallow up Jonah. And Jonah was in the belly of the fish three days and three nights."

PASTOR NEWMAN: You see that Jonah's disobedience didn't catch the Lord unaware. His providence anticipated the prophet's actions and prepared for them. I suggest you read the entire account. Contemplate your own choices. Like Jonah, if you flee God's will, you may be a danger to others wherever you go. Who knows what the cost may be if your Heavenly Father must reach out in love and chasten you back to Himself?

DAVID: I doubt God concerns Himself with one as unimportant as me.

PASTOR NEWMAN: Oh, but your Heavenly Father does concern Himself intimately with His chosen messenger, with His message, and with the men He desires to receive it—that's what you'll find in the Book of Jonah. I will pray for safety for you and those around you, and I promise that my door will always be open for you, David, when you're ready to accept God's call.

MUSIC: Piano out

(PASTOR NEWMAN leaves DAVID standing alone. DAVID is stunned and looks at the letter PASTOR NEWMAN handed him.)

NARRATOR 1: David struggled within himself, shaken by Pastor Newman's counsel. A storm of conviction raged in his heart. He knew what Pastor Newman said was true, but could not yield to it.

NARRATOR 2: The letter from his father made it worse.

NARRATOR 3: David, already angry toward God, now felt a strange anger toward his father as well, for allowing all this to happen. His troubled thoughts were interrupted by his aunt's cheerful voice.

(AUNT ABIGAIL calls from off stage.)

AUNT ABIGAIL: Davy, come by the fire and join with us in a carol.

(DAVID bows his head, exits)

MUSIC: "Come, Thou Long Expected Jesus"

PART THREE: THE FLIGHT
Scene One: Trent Farm Outside Newport
Early Christmas Morning

(The stage is the deck of a ship. DAVID, MARCUS stand with heads bowed.)

NARRATOR 1: *(Audible cue for NARRATOR CHORUS)*

NARRATOR CHORUS:

"But Jonah rose up to flee from the presence of the Lord,

    and went down to Joppa;

    And he found a ship going to Tarshish:

    So he paid the fare thereof,

    and went down into it,

    to go with them to Tarshish

    from the presence of the LORD." (Jonah 1:3)

NARRATOR 1: Aunt Abigail, Pastor Newman, and the other guests enjoyed themselves around the hearth. They sang several other carols and read the nativity story from the Gospels of Matthew and Luke.

NARRATOR 2: And Aunt Abigail coaxed Pastor Newman into sharing a thrilling first-hand account of crossing the Delaware with Washington's desperate army, that snowy Christmas Day in 1776, and the ensuing capture of Trenton.

NARRATOR 3: David sat privately brooding in a cold corner farthest away from the fire and the festivity. No merry Christmas for him. Everything about Christmas disturbed him that night, reminding him of his call to preach the gospel.

NARRATOR 1: A desperate, nervous energy built inside him, a

rising urge to get away from Christmas and all it entailed. As soon as it was polite to do so, he bid his aunt and her guests good night and went to his room.

NARRATOR 2: But he didn't go to bed. He dashed off a brief note to his aunt, a lie about visiting Marcus. He gathered a few of his things and most of the money his uncle had left him. He slipped out the back, saddled his horse, and hurried down the dark, snowy road, nine miles to Newport.

NARRATOR 1: By prearrangement, David rapped on Marcus's window and roused him at his grandparents' farm.

DAVID: *(Whispering)* You ready to leave?

MARCUS: *(Whispering back)* You really are serious about this, aren't you?

DAVID: I'm going whether you come along or not.

MARCUS: What about my tools?

DAVID: Leave them. They'll slow us down. We'll buy what you need when we get to Paris.

MARCUS: Give me a few minutes to gather clothes, then.

DAVID: Hurry! Hasseltine's sailing at sunrise. I must be aboard!

MARCUS: Meet you in front!

NARRATOR 2: David led his horse around the house to the front porch. He halted when he saw what awaited him there. Nancy stood out on the cold porch.

(NANCY steps out, arms folded across her chest in a stern expression of displeasure)

NARRATOR 3: Putting God out of his mind put Nancy out too, and he was prepared for this confrontation.

DAVID: *(Thinking fast)* I . . . I brought you this horse as a

Christmas present.

NANCY: I don't want your horse or anything else aiding in your plans.

DAVID: What plans?

NANCY: You didn't come bringing a gift. You're running away.

DAVID *(At a loss for what to say)* I . . . I . . . .

NANCY: Please don't run away, Davy! I know it's bold for a young female to talk this way, but there's no time, so I'll be blunt: I'd begun to hope that there would be much more between us, but not now.

DAVID: Maybe there could be some day.

NANCY: Not if you're running off to France.

DAVID: Perhaps I'll send for you in time.

NANCY: I won't come. Not in time. Not ever.

DAVID: I'll go on writing to you.

NANCY: I won't read your letters anymore.

DAVID: I thought you'd begun to care for me.

NANCY: I do care *(voice choking)* more than you realize. *(Tears welling up)* That's why I won't come to you or even read your letters. I've dedicated my life to serving the Lord Jesus Christ and have been praying for a young man with that same dedication. After we'd talked in Providence, and as I read your past correspondence—how your heart had been opening to God— I felt you might be him for whom I've prayed. I'd hoped there might be a future for us together someday, but in serving the Lord, not running from Him.

(MARCUS enters carrying a carpet bag.)

DAVID: Marcus, what on earth did you tell her?

MARCUS: Sorry, Davy. She ran into Robert Thacker, one of your college friends, in town the other day, and asked about you. She wheedled the rest out of me when she came home.

NANCY: David Youngman, I'll go anywhere with you serving the Lord—to the Indians, the West Indies, or far-away India—but I'm going to draw near to God, not run from Him. I'll be waiting here with your horse, praying for you to turn back to the Lord again.

DAVID: Then it's goodbye, Nancy.

NANCY: I can't say farewell, only "Don't run away!"

(DAVID exits)

MARCUS: Goodbye, Nan.

NANCY: I should be angry with you, Marcus, for being part of this, but Davy needs someone to watch out for him. You take care. And take care of Davy for me, please!

MARCUS: I'll try.

(NANCY exits, sobbing softly. MARCUS is rejoined by DAVID. They stand with bowed heads and are joined by CAPT. HASSELTINE during the following narration.)

Scene Two: Aboard the Merchant Ship *Pocassett* Christmas Day

NARRATOR 1: The two young men hurried into the sleeping town and headed to the docks.

NARRATOR 3: The seaport lay quiet in the frosty air. Only one ship bustled with activity as dawn showed crimson beyond the island.

(DAVID, MARCUS, and CAPT. HASSELTINE raise their heads.)

DAVID: *(Calling to him on the ship)* Merry Christmas, Captain Hasseltine!

MARCUS: Merry Christmas!

HASSELTINE: Merry Christmas, my lads! Come to see me off, or come to sail with me?

DAVID: To sail with you today!

MARCUS: Despite the blockade.

HASSELTINE: Well, that's the spirit if you want to get ahead in this world! Come aboard, my lads. Welcome aboard the good ship Pocassett. Get you up on the quarter-deck there. Ask for Mr. Lattimore, my first mate. He'll sign you in on the ship's log, collect your fare, and have our cabin boy show you accommodations, such as we have.

NARRATOR 1: As the rising sun gleams above the eastern hills, the hands weigh anchor and hoist sails. In honor of the day, they sing a Christmas carol as they work.

MUSIC: "I Heard The Herald Angels Sing On Christmas Day In The Morning" *(See Production Notes for the words. A men's group would be good here, as if they were the sailors singing a rousing Christmas song.)*

NARRATOR 3: The Pocassett glided like a dream from the quay and headed out to sea. The cries of the gulls, the swift ship plunging through the waves, and the brisk ocean breeze all numbed the cares of David's heart.

NARRATOR 2: The snowy Rhode Island shoreline disappeared behind them. Weary from inner struggles and traveling through the night down the island to Newport, David headed below and fell into a deep sleep.

NARRATOR 3: Everything peaceful and calm; David slept through the morning and into the early afternoon.

HASSELTINE: *(Strains to see some distant object off the bow, then calls)* All hands on deck! *(Puts telescope to his eye and scans the horizon in front of his ship again, fixing on what he saw. He gives orders to the unseen helmsman.)* Hard to starboard! Change course, south by so'west, to those clouds building there.

MARCUS: *(Concerned)* Something wrong, Captain?

HASSELTINE: *(Looking through a telescope)* Sail off the port bow and closing fast.

MARCUS: *(Straining to see with his own eyes)* Another merchant ship? Fishermen? A whaler, perhaps?

CAPT. HASSELTINE: Too fast! Bet my life it's that nasty British frigate! Had their spies back in Newport, no doubt. *(Calling to the deck)* Hands aloft! All sails, ta'gallants and stun'sils! Shake out every inch of canvas! *(Gloating)* We'll give 'em a merry Christmas chase!

MARCUS: Can they catch you?

HASSELTINE: Ha! The Pocassett's swift! And I know a trick or two. *(looks to the bow)* Storm coming up from the southwest. We'll lose him running towards it.

NARRATOR 2: The wind sang through the taut ropes as the Pocassett raced ahead, and the sails behind diminished a bit in size.

HASSELTINE: That's showing 'em!

NARRATOR 1: Everything went smoothly, distance increasing every moment, until a thunderous, jolting crash ended their flight.

SFX: *Broken timber cracking.* *Shouts of "Look out!" The sound like a large tree falling, followed by a tremendous crash of debris on deck.*

MARCUS: *(shocked)* What's happened?!

HASSELTINE: *(Striking his leg in frustration)* Merry Christmas, indeed! We've lost our main mast, and it's fouled other rigging! *(Perplexed)* Never seen the like before. How could this happen? A fair wind and following sea, yet it's like the hand of God reached down and snapped the mast like a twig! *(Looking back toward the British, with despair)* They'll have us now.

NARRATOR 2: Swift and inexorable, the distant sail swept in.

SFX: Distant Cannon Shot

NARRATOR 1: A dull boom, a momentary puff of smoke, and a nearby splash as the man o' war fired across their bow, signaling them to surrender.

HASSELTINE: *(Frustrated)* As if he needs us to heave to. We're already dead in the water. Now he'll have his way with us.

NARRATOR 3: The frigate hove to a short distance away, gun ports bristling with cannons, and marines with their muskets aloft in the rigging.

LT. STURNDALE: *(Off-stage voice yelling through cupped hands)* Ahoy! Stand by to be boarded!

NARRATOR 1: A longboat was already pulling across, and it came alongside. A dozen red-coated marines, bayonets ready, poured onto the deck, followed by a score of sailors with naked cutlasses.

NARRATOR 3: A moment later, two dour officers in blue uniforms, swords in hand, climbed aboard.

(CAPT. FORESTER and LT. STURNDALE enter to one side.)

CAPT. FORESTER: *(Looking the damaged ship over with a professional eye)* I'm Captain Richard Forester of His Britannic Majesty's frigate, Leviathan. My first officer, Mr. Sturndale.

HASSELTINE: Captain Edward Hasseltine of the merchantman Pocassett. What business is this stopping an American ship in American waters?!

CAPT. FORESTER: *(Grim, businesslike, ignoring Hasseltine's question)* Mr. Sturndale, check their log. I want every man listing an English town as his origin.

LT. STURNDALE: Aye, sir.

NARRATOR 2: Hasseltine's crewmen were herded together on the deck. David was roughly tumbled out of bed and forced at sword point to join them.

LT. STURNDALE: *(As if holding up a piece of paper)* Copied 'em from the ship's log, sir. These are the names and places.

CAPT. FORESTER: *(Looking the paper over)* Ha hmm. These 13 men appear to be British subjects. They will be taken into the service of their king. *(Hands the list back)*

HASSELTINE: I must protest, sir!

CAPT. FORESTER: I've no time to waste on feeble protests! The Royal Navy struggles with the Corsican Tyrant, and I'll take every able-bodied Englishman for my crew.

MARCUS: Not me!

DAVID: Captain Hasseltine, what about us?

HASSELTINE: Those two young men are paid passengers.

CAPT. FORESTER: Their names?

DAVID: David Youngman.

MARCUS: Marcus Trent.

LT. STURNDALE: *(Checking list)* Youngman, Trent. The log lists "Portsmouth" as their origin.

CAPT. FORESTER: Portsmouth, England, we'll assume.

DAVID: No! Portsmouth, Rhode Island!

MARCUS: We're Americans!

LT. STURNDALE: Silence! *(to FORESTER)* Sir! Shall I bring over a prize crew?

CAPT. FORESTER: No. There'll be no sailing her to Halifax today. Too much wreckage to clear with this storm coming on. Take the new men over as soon as the rice is thrown overboard.

LT. STURNDALE: Aye, sir!

HASSELTINE: Overboard?! This is an outrage!

CAPT. FORESTER: Hasseltine, you're the outrage, flaunting our blockade again and again! But not this time. Be thankful I don't send this vessel to the bottom of the sea. *(Glances up at the damaged rigging)* By the looks of your rigging, Providence has done a work for us this day. We'll leave you to Divine Mercy and the storm.

(DAVID and MARCUS exit ahead of FORESTER and STURNDALE)

HASSELTINE: Of all the foul luck! I'm ruined! Ruined! *(He exits the opposite way.)*

Scene Three: On Board *H.M.S. Leviathan*
Christmas Week

NARRATOR 1: *(Audible cue)*

NARRATOR CHORUS:

"Now the LORD had prepared a great fish to swallow up Jonah . . ." (Jonah 1:17)

(DAVID and MARCUS enter with GEORGE and HARRY. CAPT. FORESTER and LT. STURNDALE follow and stand slightly apart.)

NARRATOR 2: David, Marcus, and other unfortunate men were forced at gunpoint to haul heavy grain sacks up from the hold and pitch them over the side.

SFX: Thunder

NARRATOR 3: By the time they finished, the storm was almost upon them. Thunder rumbled nearby as they rowed across the rising waves to the British vessel.

CAPT. FORESTER: Mr. Sturndale, read them the Articles of War and enter them into the ship's log.

LT. STURNDALE: Aye, sir.

CAPT. FORESTER: Then put 'em to work battening down for the storm. Let's see who the true sailors are among them.

(The men stand with heads bowed until after the NARRATORS describe)

NARRATOR 1: Lt. Sturndale read the Articles of War in a droning voice. The conduct regulations shocked David as he heard of the many infractions that could bring flogging or even death to an offender.

NARRATOR 2: Immediately after the reading, the new men were compelled to labor on the deck, preparing for the storm. The boson's mate applied a rattan cane to the backsides of those failing to move quickly or perform to his expectations. He is roughest on David and Marcus.

NARRATOR 3: As soon as he could, David tried reasoning with the first officer.

(DAVID, MARCUS, and STURNDALE raise their heads.)

DAVID: Sir, there's been a terrible mistake. I'm no sailor. I'm a student.

MARCUS: I'm only a cobbler.

LT. STURNDALE: *(Mocking in disbelief)* A student? Only a cobbler? Enough with you! Back to work!

NARRATOR 1: A rude beginning to a harsh existence. Members of the crew stripped David of his uncle's pocket watch and his money pouch. The work was hard and dangerous, and the discipline merciless. David and Marcus were forced to climb the rigging and adjust the sails. Any hesitation brought curses from an angry boson and a sharp stroke from his rattan.

NARRATOR 3: Below decks, they found little consolation. The men slept in tiers of hammocks stacked four high and barely 18 inches apart. The foul air reeked of cooking and unwashed bodies.

NARRATOR 2: So long at sea, much of the ship's perishable food grew rancid. The drinking water tasted stale and bitter from being so long in a wooden cask.

NARRATOR 3: Finally, after spending Christmas afternoon in arduous toil, David and Marcus sat down to a cheerless meal.

(DAVID and MARCUS raise their heads along with GEORGE and HARRY. Note: GEORGE and HARRY speak with a rough Cockney-like dialect and are meant to be played for whatever humor comes from those characters, dark as that humor may be.)

HARRY: (Mocking tone) H'enjoying yer Christmas dinner, lads?

GEORGE: (Mocking tone) Aww! We's fresh out of roast goose an' plum puddin'.

HARRY: But 'ere's peas porridge an' salt pork to make up fer it!

(HARRY and GEORGE laugh at their jest)

DAVID: (Holding up an imaginary object the size of a hockey puck) What's this supposed to be?

GEORGE: Ship's biscuit, mate.

(HARRY is tapping a hard, hockey puck-shaped object on the table with one hand.)

MARCUS: Biscuit? It's more like a rock.

GEORGE: H'ain't no Christmas tea cake!

MARCUS: Why are you tapping it on the table that way?

HARRY: (Laughs at them) Brings out the weevils a'fore eatin'.

GEORGE: Don't go gnawin' at it dry. Yew soak whut's left in yer grub.

HARRY: Otherwise yew'll break off all your teeth like ol' George' ere.

GEORGE: Not all! Two or three still there!

MARCUS: Davy, what's happened to us?

DAVID: I'm afraid to think of it, Marcus.

(HARRY, and GEORGE laugh cruelly at them before DAVID, MARCUS, HARRY, and GEORGE bow their heads)

NARRATOR 3: The storm blasted fully upon them. Tremendous waves tossed the vessel about, adding to hardship and discomfort. There was no trying to sleep.

NARRATOR 1: Accidents the following day injured several men, always when David was around.

NARRATOR 2: David worked with a gang securing stores in the dim light of the hold. The tossing ship lurched suddenly in a rogue wave. A heavy barrel broke free and crashed against a stanchion, injuring three men as its staves gave way, wasting precious gallons of drinking water.

NARRATOR 3: When David labored on his hands and knees scouring the galley deck, a rat tipped over a nearby lantern, spilling the lamp oil and causing a small fire, a great danger on a wooden ship. Two men burned themselves while helping to douse the flames.

NARRATOR 2: Later, when David was on the main deck refastening the longboat tarpaulin, chains securing a nearby gun carriage suddenly snapped. The cannon rumbled freely around the pitching deck, crashing into bulkheads, wounding four men, and dismounting two other heavy cannons before it could be stopped.

NARRATOR 1: The crew grew restless with the mounting casualties. Bellow decks, they grumbled and eyed David with suspicion. They sensed an unknown something connecting him to all the accidents.

(HARRY, GEORGE, and MARCUS raise their heads)

GEORGE: 'Ey, mate, whut's wit yer chum?

MARCUS: What do you mean?

HARRY: 'E's a rum bloke, tha' one. Everywhere 'e's workin', bad things seems ta 'appen.

MARCUS: Nonsense. I've known him for years.

GEORGE: 'E's pure bad luck, if yew ask me.

HARRY: Aye! Regular "Jonah," 'e is!

GEORGE: Steer clear of 'im or yew'll be next, mate!

(GEORGE, HARRY, and MARCUS bow their heads)

NARRATOR 3: Night fell again, leaving everyone on edge. Tensions rose as the ocean storm intensified even more.

SFX: A storm at sea, howling wind, in the background through this scene.

(FORESTER and STURNDALE raise their heads)

CAPT. FORESTER: (above the wind) What a night!

LT. STURNDALE: (above the wind) Captain, I've never seen such a storm!

CAPT. FORESTER: Unusual, even for winter.

LT. STURNDALE: It's as if God were hounding this ship.

CAPT. FORESTER: If I were a theologian, I'd agree with you. (Looking way up and noticing that the top gallant sails have come loose) Top gallants have come loose again. This wind will shred 'em for sure. Send hands aloft to secure ta'gallants.

LT. STURNDALE: Aye, sir. (Calling to the crew) Hands aloft! Secure ta'gallant s'ils!

(DAVID and MARCUS raise their heads.)

MARCUS: *(above the wind)* "Secure ta'gallant s'ils?" What's that supposed to mean?

DAVID: *(above the wind)* It means climb up and tie the top gallant sails. Start climbing before the angry boson comes with his cane!

MARCUS: *(above the wind)* Up there in this wind and rain?!

DAVID: *(above the wind)* Quick, here he comes!

NARRATOR 1: Lightning flashed as David and Marcus struggled up the rigging. They slipped on the wet ropes and swayed in the gusty wind.

MARCUS: *(Climbing, calling)* Where are the ta'gallant s'ils?

DAVID: *(Climbing, calling)* At the very top. Almost there!

MARCUS: *(desperate)* Davy, Help! I'm slipping!

DAVID: *(Calling)* Hang on, I'm coming!

MARCUS: *(In terror as he falls)* Davy!

DAVID: *(In horror)* Marcus!

(MARCUS turns his back toward the audience as he bows out. DAVID bows his head.)

NARRATOR 1: *(audible cue for NARRATOR CHORUS)*

NARRATOR CHORUS:

"And they said every one to his fellow,

'Come, and let us cast lots,

that we may know for whose cause this evil is upon us.'

So they cast lots, and the lot fell upon Jonah." (Jonah 1:7)

NARRATOR 3: Grief-stricken, David finally returned to his hammock. He grieved for Marcus, lying close to death in the sick bay, and sorrowed for himself, unaware of the sailors crouched in a dark corner, rolling dice.

(MARCUS exits as HARRY and GEORGE raise their heads)

GEORGE: Roll again, mate. The dice'll confirm it!

HARRY: *(Rolls his dice, and interprets the results.)* The new bloke in the 'ammock. 'Tis 'im for sure.

GEORGE: Figgered so. *(Sneering)* The student!

HARRY: Can't just slit 'is throat. Make it look like a fight.

GEORGE: H'eas'ly done!

NARRATOR 1: The rough sailor took out his knife and cut the rope at one end of David's hammock. David tumbled down onto the deck.

(DAVID raises his head abruptly, rubbing his bruised skull.)

DAVID: Hey! What is this?!

GEORGE: *(Holding his knife low and menacingly)* All right, mate. This 'ere ship 'as been dogged by bad luck e're since we took on yer lot.

HARRY: We've rolled the dice an' 'tis yew they picked.

GEORGE: H'it's yew whut brung this bad luck on us.

HARRY: H'it's yew whut caused yer friend to fall, prob'ly die.

GEORGE: But we knows 'ow to git rid of "Jonahs" like yew!

(STURNDALE raises his head quickly)

LT. STURNDALE: *(Angrily demanding)* What is going on here?!

GEORGE: *(Quickly blaming DAVID)* H'it's 'is fault, sir. Tried to pick a fight with me an 'arry.

HARRY: Pulled a knife on us, but George' ere took it away.

DAVID: That's a lie!

LT. STURNDALE: Bring him along. He's been trouble ever since he came aboard.

NARRATOR 2: Rough hands hauled David before Captain Forester.

(FORESTER *raises his head*)

CAPT. FORESTER: (*Cold anger*) You've been on board less than 48 hours and nothing but trouble. Why have you plagued my ship? There must be a reason! Are you in the pay of the French? Tell me plainly!

DAVID: I've been running from the call of God.

NARRATOR 1: Stunned silence. Everyone knew David spoke the truth.

CAPT. FORESTER: (*With loathing*) For this "running" of yours, you've brought danger to everyone aboard this vessel, and your friend barely lives!

DAVID: (*Filled with remorse*) Everything's my fault. The accidents, the storm, and Marcus falling—all because I disobeyed and fled God's commission to preach the Gospel. I deserve to be thrown into the sea!

CAPT. FORESTER: I'll throw you into the brig instead, while I determine what to do with your wretched hide! Take him away!

(FORESTER *and* STURNDALE *exit while* HARRY, GEORGE *bring* DAVID *to his seat and exit leaving* DAVID *sitting alone.*)

NARRATOR 3: Rough hands shove David into the brig. Rougher hands clasp him in irons. The lamp is blown out. The door slams shut.

(*Pause for SFX to run a few seconds*)

SFX: *Ship Creaking* fades back in and then slowly out

beneath narration.

NARRATOR 1: There David sits—alone, miserable, and full of sorrow in the darkness.

(DAVID sobs quietly)

NARRATOR 2: Time seems to stand still. David weeps for Marcus until no more tears come, and then he sadly ponders each bitter step, each selfish decision.

NARRATOR 1: He knows God directed every disaster that has befallen since he fled.

DAVID: *(To himself)* God appointed a fish to swallow Jonah, and now He's appointed the Royal Navy to deal with me.

(DAVID bows in prayer and holds in place during Narration and MUSIC

NARRATOR 1: *(audible cue for NARRATOR CHORUS)*

NARRATOR CHORUS:

"Then Jonah prayed unto the LORD his God out of the fish's belly." (Jonah 2:1)

MUSIC: The Piano plays "Thou Didst Leave Thy Throne" softly, slowly in the background while DAVID speaks

DAVID: *(Raises his head, looking upward as if addressing God)* Almighty, Merciful God, I thank You that You control the wind and the waves. You guide the storms, both the ones at sea and the ones in the hearts of men.

I've sinned by rejecting Your call to me. I've hated those You love and gave Your Son to die for. I've endangered others and brought Marcus near death. I can't flee from Your presence. You remained with me everywhere my running away has led me, even to this horrible prison.

O Lord, forgive my great sin. I now yield to Your call. Release me from the bondage of my hate. I forgive those who slew my parents, just as I know You forgive me my trespasses through Jesus Christ. Grant me the grace now to bring the light of Thy Gospel to people who walk in darkness.

Please heal Marcus and the other crewmen as well. Have mercy on all aboard this ship now. Please set me free from this brig and send me on the way to doing Your will. Amen.

(DAVID bows his head during song and beginning of the EPILOGUE)

MUSIC: "Thou Didst Leave Thy Throne" now is
sung.

EPILOGUE
Scene: Off Martha's Vineyard
Late December

*SFX: **Distant Sea gulls, gentle waves** gradually fading out under dialogue.*

NARRATOR 1: *(audible cue for NARRATOR CHORUS)*

NARRATOR CHORUS:

> ". . . And the sea ceased from her raging.
>
> Then the men feared the LORD exceedingly . . .and made vows." *(Jonah 1:15-16)*

(FORESTER and STURNDALE enter.)

LT. STURNDALE: Sir, have you noticed how unusually calm it's been these last three days?

CAPT. FORESTER: Yes. Heavenly after that horrendous storm.

LT. STURNDALE: Sir, what shall we do with the man in the brig?

CAPT. FORESTER: I'm pondering him, too. I've not been much of a religious man, but it seems obvious, even to me, that God's hand has been in all of the trouble.

LT. STURNDALE: Reminds me uncannily like the book of Jonah, sir, from the Old Testament.

CAPT. FORESTER: Aye, that! An eerie similarity, to be sure. And his injured friend, still making progress after he regained consciousness?

LT. STURNDALE: Remarkable, miraculous even. Ship's surgeon

can't account for the speed of the man's recovery. This morning, he reports only a broken arm and a knot on the man's head to show for the fall.

CAPT. FORESTER: I've seen others fall from that height. None survived. Why not this fellow?

LT. STURNDALE: Trick of the wind, perhaps, maybe bringing him down from sheet to sheet, landing him the way he did on the long boat tarpaulin, but even that's the mercy of God, sir.

CAPT. FORESTER: God again. God in everything, it seems! *(Pondering)* Ha-hmmm. Everything going from bad to worse, and now the opposite after we threw that "Jonah" into the brig.

LT. STURNDALE: If you don't mind my saying, sir, he ought to stand before the mast and receive due punishment under the Articles of War for endangering the safety of this vessel.

CAPT. FORESTER: No. A Greater Authority than the Articles of War is involved. Beyond the Almighty's hand, I can't explain what's been happening aboard this ship. Call it the Holy Spirit or an old sailor's intuition, I feel a strong compulsion to cast this "Jonah" and those associated with him away from us as quickly as possible.

(Looking out to the horizon, focusing on a distant spot) We're off the island they call Martha's Vineyard. *(Thinking)* Ha hmmm. *(Short pause, coming to a decision)* Set course for the island. Gather a boat's crew, the sergeant, and six marines among them. Prepare the longboat.

LT. STURNDALE: Aye, sir!

CAPT. FORESTER: Bring up the prisoner, his injured friend, and the eleven others impressed from the *Pocassett*. Restore all their belongings and anything our crew has taken—I'm sure they'll gladly give it back. Row the blighters ashore. Leave them outside the village, *(he points or nods toward it)* there.

LT. STURNDALE: All of 'em? Begging your pardon, sir, but, except for the prisoner and his injured friend, we need the rest of those men in the king's service on this ship.

CAPT. FORESTER: No, every last one <u>must</u> go. A King higher even than His Britannic Majesty desires service from that man in the brig. For the sake of this vessel, and His Majesty's Navy, we must clear ourselves of that . . . that disobedient preacher . . . and ALL associated with him. I only hope his days as a "Jonah" have come to an end. At least I can make it so, as far as this ship is concerned.

LT. STURNDALE: Very well, sir; then, good riddance, I say!

CAPT. FORESTER: *(Gravely cautioning)* Ah! But treat them well . . . and get away swiftly, lest Providence deals with us once more!

LT. FORESTER: *(Saluting)* Aye, sir! The Fear of the Lord is upon us all!

CAPT. FORESTER: *(Returning salute)* Amen! *(pronounced Ah-men, like the closing of a formal prayer.)*

(FORESTER and LT. STURNDALE bow heads momentarily through the Bible verse quotation.

NARRATOR 1: *(Audible cue for NARRATOR CHORUS)*

NARRATOR CHORUS:

"And the LORD spoke to the fish,

and it vomited out Jonah upon the dry land." (Jonah 2:10)

(Slight pause as DAVID stands and FORESTER and STURNDALE begin to exit.)

NARRATOR 1: *(Audible cue, if needed, as NARRATOR CHORUS continues)*

NARRATOR CHORUS:

"And the word of the LORD came unto Jonah the second time, saying,

'Arise, go to Nineveh, that great city,

and preach unto it the preaching I bid thee.'" (Jonah 3:2)

(DAVID looks out with peace of mind and a clear vision of the way ahead of him)

NARRATOR 1: David waits beside Marcus on the shore while the others seek help in the village a short distance away. After a while, a wagon comes rumbling toward them along the rocky beach.

NARRATOR 3: Soon, he'll bring Marcus back to Newport. Then he'll see Nancy again and ask her forgiveness. And then he'll go on, preparing for the ministry under Pastor Newman while finishing at the university, and then . . .

DAVID: *(Resolving this to himself)* . . . and then traveling west to the frontier, loving a people as God loves them, as my father and mother loved them before me, and preaching to them the glorious Gospel of my Savior, Jesus Christ.

(DAVID slowly exits, perhaps up the midde aisle of the auditorium, as NARRATORS continue)

NARRATOR 2: With tremendous peace in his soul, David walks behind the wagon toward the village, humming a Christmas carol to himself as a song of surrender. Although he's a few days late, David feels the joy of Christmas once more.

NARRATOR 1: *(Audible cue for NARRATOR CHORUS if needed.)*

NARRATOR CHORUS:

"So Jonah arose, and went unto Nineveh, according to the word of the LORD. . ." (Jonah 3:3)

MUSIC: "Joy To The World"

THE END

PRODUCTION NOTES
FOR "THE CHRISTMAS RUNAWAY"

List of Music Suggested for Use in This Program

It is suggested to use Christmas music written before the 1811 (if possible) setting of this drama. Most of the music listed below fits that time period.

1. "As With Gladness, Men Of Old"

2. A festive carol or traditional holiday song written before 1811, such as "Deck the Halls" or "The Holly and the Ivy"

3. "O Holy Night"

4. "Depth Of Mercy" by Charles Wesley or some other period hymn which might fit a missions or Christian service theme

5. "Come, Thou Long Expected Jesus"

6. "I Heard the Herald Angels Sing on Christmas Day in the Morning"

Sung to the tune of "I Saw Three Ships Come Sailing In," but with a more Scriptural text, words adapted from Charles Wesley's "Hark, The Herald Angels Sing."

I heard the herald angels sing
The angels sing, the angels sing!
All glory to the New Born King!
On Christmas Day in the morning!

And peace on Earth and mercy mild;
And mercy mild, and mercy mild!
God with all sinners reconciled,
On Christmas Day in the morning!

Now joyful all ye nations rise;
Ye nations rise, ye nations rise!
To join the triumph of the skies,
On Christmas Day in the morning!

And with angelic hosts proclaim,
With hosts proclaim, with hosts proclaim!
That Christ is born in Bethlehem,
On Christmas Day in the morning!

(adapt more from other verses as needed to fit your arrangement.)

7. "Thou Didst Leave Thy Throne"

8. "Joy To The World!"

There are also places indicated in the script where a piano or organ may play softly in the background enhancing the mood of the drama, soft enough not to interfere with dialog or narration.

List of Suggested Sound Effects

1. Creaking of a Wooden Ship (used more than once)

2. Broken timber cracking. Shouts of "Look out!" The sound like

   a Large Tree Falling, followed by a Tremendous Crash of

   Debris on deck

3. Distant Cannon Shot

4. Thunder

5. A Storm at Sea, Howling Wind

6. Distant Sea Gulls, Gentle Waves

Many sound effects are available to sample and purchase On Line, such as the BBC Sound Effects Archive and the CBS Audio-File Sound Effects library. Sometimes a public library may have them on CD.

STAGING

This drama was originally written for performance in a modified Readers Theatre style due to space constraints on the church platform where it premiered. It may also be performed in a more traditional style, with the actors interacting, while the NARRATORS are positioned off to one side. Feel free to adapt it to your needs and situation.

COSTUMING

Following the Readers Theatre style, the main characters would wear variations of long sleeved turtle neck tops and dark slacks for the men and long dark skits for the ladies. Colors could be varied. For example, the ROBERT and SIMON could be dressed in brown, DAVID in gray, NANCY and AUNT ABIGAIL in a light color, British sailors in navy or dark blue, NARRATORS in black, etc.

Although technically this drama is set in the Georgian Period between the Colonial and actual Victorian period, Victorian-style clothing will work okay if you wish to dress the characters in full costumes. See Costuming section in the Production Notes for "A Christmas Carol" for ideas.

The shipboard scenes take place aboard the *Pocasset*, an American merchant vessel, and aboard *H.M.S. Leviathan,* a frigate of the Royal Navy during the Napoleonic Wars. Watch the Horatio Hornblower movie or miniseries for other costume ideas.

Historical Background Notes:

This story is set in late 1811 amid the rising hostilities between the United States and the British Empire. These hostilities eventually led to an open declaration of war by President Madison and the Congress six months later.

The Royal Navy and American Shipping
Before and after the Revolutionary War, the British government has a low regard for America and its citizens They never consider Americans as equals (The original words and intent of the song "Yankee Doodle" reflect this, mocking the American "Yankee" for his lack of refinement, culture, and sophistication). This superior attitude, based on class distinctions in the British hierarchal society at the time, was one of the reasons behind the tyranny leading to the Declaration of Independence thirty-five years before. Attitudes toward Americans have not changed and even grow worse. Festering hard feelings following the embarrassing British defeat at Yorktown in 1781 compound that disrespect.

The world's greatest naval power at the time, the Royal Navy intimidates and impedes American commerce on the seas. Struggling against Napoleon's empire, the British maintain a blockade preventing trade with French-controlled Continental Europe.

American ships are routinely stopped and searched for contraband cargo. Blockade-runners, outwitting and eluding the British Navy, can make handsome profits transporting goods into French ports where military supplies and scarce consumer goods such as coffee, sugar and rice sell at inflated prices.

Impressment
American sailors themselves are also in peril. Because of man power shortages due to the European war, the British Navy follows a practice of "impressment" at home and on the seas. Wherever they can, the navy captures and forces able-bodied men into their service when regular recruitment fails. American sailors are attractive prizes in this policy. Differences between American dialects and culture at this time and those of the British are often only slight. Many of the sailors are former British subjects who emigrated to America and serve on American merchant vessels. Claims of American citizenship and protection under international maritime law fall on deaf ears.

Once impressed into the Royal Navy and under the harsh discipline of the Articles of War, life is virtual slavery. Desertion or mutiny carry death sentences. Even minor offenses often result in floggings. Maritime issues such as this are among those leading to an official declaration of war by President Madison and the United States Congress and the start of the War of 1812 in July of that year.

Ministry Preparation
Studying for the ministry was different at this time, six years before the founding of the first Baptist seminary in America. Traditionally among the Baptists, being outside the established state churches, men entering the ministry would usually study under an established pastor in an "apprenticeship in the ministry" situation. Baptists followed this pattern for centuries going back to Timothy and others assisting and learning under the Apostle Paul.

Those men able to attend a college or a university might receive undergraduate training before or during their time of serving under a pastor. There were no Bible colleges like today, but Biblical moral philosophy and a Judeo-Christian world view were the basis of the standard curriculum of all major colleges in the American Colonies at the time of their founding. Students also studied both classical languages (Latin and Greek) and modern languages (such as French, German and Italian).

Brown University
The first college favoring Baptists in America was in Rhode Island, the colony founded, in part, by Baptists. "The College of the English Colony of Rhode Island and Providence Plantations," was founded at Providence, Rhode Island under a royal charter in 1764. It began as a liberal arts college, providing students with a broad educational foundation (see Ministry Preparation above). In the original charter, 22 of the 36 trustees "shall forever be elected of the denomination called Baptists or Antipedobaptists"* ("Antipedobaptists" means those against infant baptism practiced by the other major denominations of that time. Baptists got their denominational name because they practiced "Believer's Baptism" after conversion). Congregationalists, Friends (Quakers) and Episcopalians divided up the remainder of the trustees. (* "Forever" lasted until 1942 when the charter was amended and denominational stipulations were removed.)

The originating charter provided that the new college could be renamed in honor of its "most distinguished donor" (something Harvard and Yale had also done). And so the school became Brown University in honor of Nicolas Brown (also one of the founders) when it changed to a university format in 1804. That same year, the university conferred an honorary doctorate on Baptist missionary William Carey for his work in India. (Carey is often called "The Father of Modern Missions" for his advocacy of overseas missionary efforts and for setting an example through his own pioneering work as a missionary himself.)

Like other early American colleges, the student body at Brown University originally was all male. Pembroke College, a separate college for women, was later founded nearby. It eventually merged with Brown University in 1971.

Brown University is one of the ten elite Ivy League Schools today. The vestiges of its Biblical world view and its Baptist roots have faded away. But in homage to its founders, the administration and the graduating class each year march in procession past the location of the Old Baptist Meeting House, the oldest existing Baptist church building in America, on their way to the annual graduation convocation. For many years that university's convocation was held in the Meeting House, at one time the largest church building in New England.

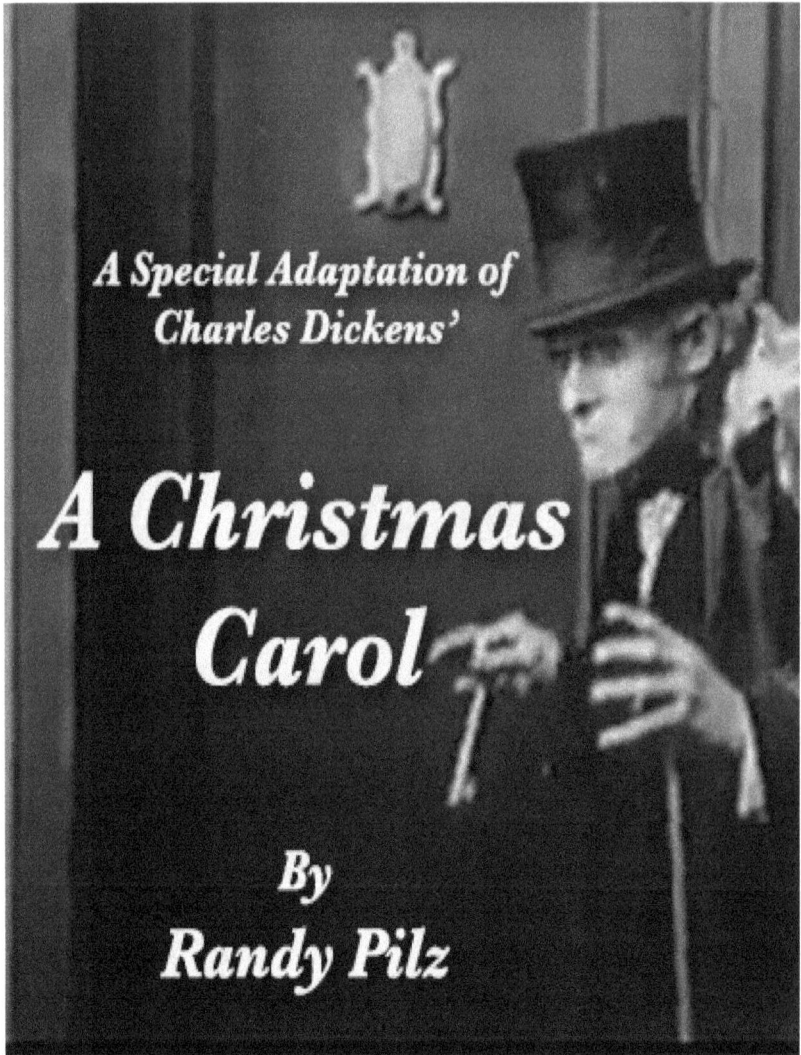

A Special Adaptation of
Charles Dickens'

A Christmas
Carol

By
Randy Pilz

A Special Adaptation of
Charles Dickens'
"A CHRISTMAS CAROL"

"Therefore if any man be in Christ,
he is a new creature:
old things are passed away;
behold, all things are become new."
2Co 5:17

Adapted by
Randy Pilz

This story appears in an expanded form,
with names and setting changed out of respect for Charles Dickens,
in the novella *The Passing Away of Chephas Steele* by Randy Pilz available at
Amazon.com

A Christmas Carol

Characters (In Order of Appearance)

NARRATOR

JOHN JENKINS—A debtor behind on his payments to SCROOGE

EBENEZER SCROOGE—a coldhearted, covetous old sinner

BOB CRATCHIT—SCROOGE'S long-suffering clerk

TWO CHARITY SOLICITORS—raising funds for the poor at Christmastime

FRED and FELICIA'S FRIENDS—out caroling on Christmas Eve afternoon

FRED—SCROOGE's cheerful nephew and the son of FAN

A CHESTNUT VENDOR—a lone street vendor still out hawking his wares

JACOB MARLEY—SCROOGE'S business partner, passed away seven years before.

FAN—SCROOGE'S beloved sister as a young woman, who died giving birth to FRED

LITTLE FAN—FAN as a child

SCROOGE, *The Lad*—SCROOGE as a lonely boarding school student

SCROOGE, *The Young Man*—SCROOGE as a young man, starting on his decline

FEZZIWIG—Kind-hearted master of SCROOGE in his younger days as an apprentice.

MRS. FEZZIWIG—Lovable wife of FEZZIWIG,

DICK WILKINS—Fellow apprentice with SCROOGE

BELLE—SCROOGE'S Fiancée and the Fezziwigs' niece

FELICIA—FRED'S delightful wife

MRS. CRATCHIT—BOB'S longsuffering wife

MARTHA CRATCHIT—Eldest Cratchit child, a factory worker in another part of the city

BELINDA CRATCHIT—Next oldest Cratchit daughter

PETER CRATCHIT—Eldest Cratchit son

TINY TIM—Youngest Cratchit, frail and sickly

TWO MERCHANTS—Business acquaintances of SCROOGE

MRS. DILBER—SCROOGE'S unscrupulous housekeeper

THE UNDERTAKER'S ASSISTANT—A despicable tradesman

OLD JOE—A shady dealer in questionable merchandise
A LAD passing by—Neighborhood lad out early on Christmas
      Morning

MUSIC and **AUDIO CUES** are marked in the script in **Bold**

Suggested Music to be played and sung and Pre-Recorded Audio to use in the drama are listed in the Production Notes

If you produce this drama in your church or school, please notify the author and let him know how things went. You may e-mail him at pilz.author@gmail.com.

THE PROGRAM

Our Program began with the children of the church. The Kindergarteners entered and sang a simple song like "Gospel Bells."

There were a lot of stings players of various levels in our church, starting with a Suzuki Strings Program on up. It is almost a tradition in that together they play "O, Come Little Children."

Other children dressed in homemade costumes as angels, shepherds, wise men, The Innn Keeper, Mary and Joseph entered singing and stood across the platform and around the front of the church and sang another song.

This was followed by announcements and the Offretory.

After the Offretory, the lights dimmed and the Choir Members entered holding battery operated candles and singing "O, Come All Ye Faithful."

Then came the Drama.

THE DRAMA

PROLOGUE

(NARRATOR enters immediately after the OFFERTORY)

MUSIC: PIANO PLAYS "I WONDER AS I WANDER" while NARRATOR enters.

NARRATOR: Charles Dickens' short novel *A Christmas Carol* is one of the most beloved stories of the season. In this delightful tale, Dickens attempted to capture the goodwill of the Christmas Spirit. He sought to present the most noble of human answers to England's increasing social dilemma, and he used supernatural ghosts to break through the protective crust of a bitter, selfish old man.

Tonight, we present a special adaptation of this story, delightfully familiar in its characterization yet markedly different in its message. As you will see, there are no ghosts in this version. Instead, a guilty conscience, a vivid dreamland imagination, and the convicting Spirit of God convince a man of his wretched condition.

Scrooge needs much more than mere human and social reformation; he needs true transformation by the grace of God. As noble as Dickens' human answer may seem, it isn't the answer at all. The real answer lies not in a man turning over a new leaf, but in a man turning to new life through salvation in Jesus Christ. For the Bible tells us, "Therefore if any man be in Christ, he is a new creature: old things are passed away; behold all things are become new."

MUSIC: Choir or Ensemble sings "O COME, O COME IMMANUEL"

NARRATOR: <u>MARLEY WAS DEAD</u>, to begin with. There is no doubt whatever about that. Scrooge knew he was dead? Of course he did. How could it be otherwise? Scrooge was his sole executor, his sole friend, and his sole mourner.

Scrooge never painted out old Marley's name. There it stood, years afterward, above the warehouse door: Scrooge and Marley. Sometimes, people new to the firm called Scrooge "Scrooge," and sometimes "Marley." But he answered to both names. It was all the same to him.

Oh, but Scrooge was a tight-fisted hand at the grindstone—A squeezing, wrenching, grasping, scraping, COVETOUS OLD SINNER! Hard and sharp as flint, secret and self-contained, and solitary as an oyster. No wind that blew was bitterer than he. He edged his way along the crowded paths of life, warning all human sympathy to keep its distance. But what did he care! IT WAS ALL THE SAME TO HIM!

(Pause)

MUSIC: WESTMINSTER CHIME CYCLE (Organ bells or orchestra chimes) sounding THREE O'CLOCK

(SCROOGE, JOHN JENKINS, CHARITY SOLICITOR, NEPHEW FRED, and the CHESTNUT VENDOR arrive during the scene; only BOB CRATCHIT moves to his seat as the chimes sound. JOHN JENKINS enters, waiting for SCROOGE. As SCROOGE briskly enters, and JOHN JENKINS moves to intercept him. MARLEY appears later in the scene.)

JOHN JENKINS: *(Humbly, nervously, with hat in hands)* Mister Scrooge . . .

(SCROOGE, absorbed in his thoughts, does not notice him at first.)

JOHN JENKINS: Mister Scrooge, sir, excuse me . . .

SCROOGE: *(Irritated)* Who are you and what do you want?

JENKINS: I'm John Jenkins, sir. It's about my loan, sir.

SCROOGE: Oh, yes, Jenkins. A loan of forty pounds, I believe.

JENKINS: I . . . I can't pay it, sir. I need more time.

SCROOGE: *(Appalled)* What do you mean, "can't pay?"

JENKINS: It's my wife, sir. She's been deathly ill. All we had went to the doctor.

SCROOGE: *(With contempt and without feeling)* You should have thought of that when you took the loan. *(Sternly)* Forty pounds is forty pounds. *(Without caring)* I'll turn you over to the magistrate.

JENKINS: *(Pleading)* I can't take my wife to debtor's prison. Please, sir! It'd kill her for sure.

SCROOGE: *(Turning away abruptly)* Humbug!

(JOHN JENKINS moves away dejectedly. SCROOGE enters the Counting House.)

STAVE ONE: MARLEY

NARRATOR: Once upon a time—of all the good days of the year, on Christmas Eve—Old Scrooge entered his counting house. The city clocks had just gone three, but it was already quite dark. It was cold, bleak, biting weather, and fog came pouring in through every chink and keyhole.

(CHARITY SOLICITORS, C.S. 1 and C.S. 2, enter and bow to BOB CRATCHIT first)

C. S. 1: *(referring to a list)* Scrooge and Marley's, I believe.

(BOB gestures him toward SCROOGE. C.S. 1 and C.S. 2 advance and bow to SCROOGE)

C.S. 1: Have we the pleasure of addressing Mr. Scrooge or Mr. Marley?

SCROOGE: Mr. Marley has been dead these seven years. He died . . . *(slight hesitation as he remembers the anniversary)* seven years ago this very night.

C.S. 2: *(Cheerfully)* No doubt his liberality is well represented by his surviving partner.

C.S. 1: At this festive season of the year, Mr. Scrooge, it is more than usually desirable that we should make some slight provision for the poor and destitute, who suffer greatly at the present time.

C.S. 2: Many thousands need common necessities, common comforts, sir.

SCROOGE: Are there no prisons?

C.S. 1: Plenty of prisons.

SCROOGE: And the Union Workhouses, are they still in operation?

C.S. 2: They are still. I wish to say they weren't.

SCROOGE: Oh! I was afraid, from what you said at first, that something had occurred to stop them in their useful course. I'm glad to hear it.

C.S. 1: Under the impression that they scarcely furnish Christian cheer of mind or body to the multitude, some of us are endeavoring to raise a fund to buy the poor some food and means of warmth and share with them the gospel of our Lord Jesus Christ.

C.S. 2: We choose this time because it's a time, of all others when Want is keenly felt and Abundance rejoices. Remember the words of our dear Savior, "Inasmuch as ye have done it unto the least of these my brethren, ye have done it unto me." What should we put you down for?

SCROOGE: Nothing!

C.S. 1: You wish to be anonymous?

SCROOGE: I wish to be left alone! I don't make merry myself at Christmas, and I can't afford to make idle people merry. I help to support the establishments I've mentioned—they cost enough, and those who are bad off must go there.

C.S. 2: *(Appalled)* Many can't go there; many would rather die.

SCROOGE: If they would rather die, they had better do it and decrease the surplus population. Good afternoon!

(Speechless, the CHARITY SOLICITORS bow and hurry out as FRED and his FRIENDS, as CAROLERS, begin moving into position, singing as they come.)

MUSIC: Ensemble as Fred and Felicia's friends sing "CAROLING, CAROLING" *(or other bright Christmas Carol)*

(The CAROLERS depart, leaving FRED, who enters SCROOGE'S office.)

FRED: Merry Christmas, Bob Cratchit!

BOB: And to you, Mr. Fred.

FRED: *(Cheerful, joking)* Is the lion in his den?

BOB: He is, sir, and he's in no good humor.

FRED: *(Laughs)* Is he ever? *(FRED prepares himself to face his uncle)* Merry Christmas, Uncle!

SCROOGE: Bah! Humbug!

FRED: *(Laughs)* Christmas a "humbug?" Uncle! You don't mean that, I'm sure?

SCROOGE: *(Growling)* I do. *(Scoffing)* Merry Christmas! What right have you to be merry? You're poor enough.

FRED: *(Gaily)* Come, then, what right have you to be dismal? You're rich enough.

SCROOGE: Bah! *(pause)* Humbug!

FRED: Don't be cross, Uncle!

SCROOGE: What else can I be when I live in such a world of fools as this? If I could work my will, every idiot who goes about with "Merry Christmas" on his lips should be boiled in his own pudding and buried with a stake of holly through his heart!

FRED: Uncle!

SCROOGE: Nephew! Keep Christmas in your own way and let me keep it in mine.

FRED: Keep it!? But you don't keep it!

SCROOGE: Let me leave it alone then.

FRED: Uncle, it's the time to remember that God loves you and sent His Son to die for you. At Christmas, we can all be thankful that "He is not willing that any should perish" and that He wants all men to come to Him in repentance.

SCROOGE: I leave God alone, and I want Him to leave me alone.

FRED: And I'm going to pray that He does not leave you alone, especially at Christmas time.

SCROOGE: "Christmas-time," humbug! What good has Christmas-time ever done you?

FRED: There are many things from which I've derived good by which I've not profited materially. I've always thought of Christmas as a loving, kind, forgiving time—a reflection of God's heart toward us—a time for us to open our hearts toward Him. *(With resolution)* Uncle, though it's never put a scrap of silver or gold in my pocket, I believe it's done me good, and will do me good, and I say, God bless it!

BOB: *(applauding)* Here, here!

(BOB CRATCHIT applauds until SCROOGE glowers at him)

SCROOGE: *(to BOB)* Let me hear another sound from you, Cratchit, and you'll keep your Christmas by losing your situation! *(CRATCHIT quickly goes back to his writing. SCROOGE returns to addressing FRED, angrily.)* You're a powerful speaker, sir. I wonder if you don't enter parliament.

FRED: Don't be angry, Uncle. Come! Dine with Felecia, me, and our friends after church tomorrow.

SCROOGE: Spend time with you and your foolish friends? Good afternoon! *(These successive "Good afternoons" increase in intensity)*

FRED: I want nothing from you. I ask nothing of you. Why can't we be friends?

SCROOGE: *(Showing him the office door)* Good afternoon!

FRED: I'm sorry to find you so resolute, but I made the trial in homage to Christmas, and I'll keep my Christmas humor to the last. A Merry Christmas, Uncle!

SCROOGE: GOOD AFTERNOON!

(FRED *steps out, then mischievously pops back in to needle his Uncle*)

FRED: And a happy new year!

SCROOGE: <u>GOOD AFTERNOON</u>! (*SCROOGE turns his back on FRED*)

FRED: *(departing)* I tried, Bob, I sincerely tried. Only God can reach that hardened heart. Let us pray that He will.

BOB: I do, sir.

FRED: How is your youngest son, the little lame boy? What is his name?

BOB: It's Timothy, but we call him "Tiny Tim," sir. He seems to be doing better right now.

FRED: Excellent. Felecia and I shall pray for him as well.

BOB: Thank you, sir. A merry Christmas to you, sir.

FRED: And to you and your family, Bob.

(FRED *exits. SCROOGE comes over to* CRATCHIT)

SCROOGE: Might as well lock up now, no one seems to be doing business anymore today with all this Christmas nonsense. I suppose you'll be wanting the whole day off tomorrow.

BOB: If it's quite convenient, sir.

SCROOGE: It's not convenient, and it's not fair. If I were to stop half a crown by it, you'd think yourself ill used, I'll be bound. And yet you don't think me ill-used when I pay a day's wages for no work.

BOB: It's only once a year.

SCROOGE: A poor excuse for picking a man's purse every twenty-fifth of December! But I suppose you must have the whole day. Be here all the earlier next morning.

BOB: I will, sir. Thank you, sir. *(starts to leave, but remembers something)* I wanted to give you this, sir, as a Christmas gift.

SCROOGE: What is this, Cratchit? Do you joke with me? This is only a printed piece of paper.

BOB: It's a gospel pamphlet. It tells how you can receive God's greatest gift, Salvation in Jesus Christ.

SCROOGE: Enough of this. Get on with you now!

BOB: *(Hurrying off)* Merry Christmas, sir!

SCROOGE: Bah! *(Looks at the pamphlet with disgust)*

(SCROOGE pauses and looks at the gospel pamphlet with disgust. He is about to tear it to bits, but the thought of wasting paper stops him.)

SCROOGE: *(muttering out loud)* It might save me tuppence to light a fire with.

(He thrusts the paper in his pocket.)

NARRATOR: Scrooge stepped out into the fog and darkness. The cold bit at his nose as he made his way through increasing gloom past a lone street vendor still out hawking his wares.

(The VENDOR enters and meets SCROOGE. The VENDOR is extremely jovial, no matter what SCROOGE says.)

VENDOR: Chestnuts! Hot Chestnuts! *(Sees SCROOGE)* Hot Chestnuts, Guv'ner? Just the thing on a cold Christmas Eve.

SCROOGE: Humbug.

VENDOR: *(Laughs heartily)* Come now, sir, where's your Christmas Spirit on this fine evening?

SCROOGE: *(Sarcastic)* I possess no Christmas Spirit, nor do I want any.

VENDOR: *(Laughs again)* Pity on you, sir. Look around you. *(Laughs)* No time like the present when there's so much to enjoy with family and friends. The whole city overflowing with happiness. Come and know it better, man! *(Laughs)*

SCROOGE: *(Sarcastic)* Come and know it better! I doubt you have aught to teach me that I can profit by.

VENDOR: *(Laughs)* Just the same, sir, come and know it better! *(Laughingly)* I can show you a Christmas the likes of which you've never seen before! It'll do you good, sir.

SCROOGE: I'll retire to Bedlam first.

VENDOR: *(Laughs)* Come now! A merry Christmas to you just the same, Guv'ner.

SCROOGE: *(Continuing on his way)* Bah!

(VENDOR exits, still calling, "Chestnuts! Hot Chestnuts!)

NARRATOR: Scrooge took his usual melancholy dinner in his usual melancholy tavern. After reading the newspapers and his banker's book, he headed for home in the fog and darkness.

Scrooge lived in gloomy chambers in a gloomy house which once belonged to his deceased partner. Having just talked of Marley's death that afternoon, Scrooge's thoughts were on Jacob Marley as he came to the door. There was a large knocker on that door, and having his key in the lock, Scrooge looked up, and for a flicker on an instant imagined in fog and gloom he saw not a door knocker but MARLEY'S FACE!

(SCROOGE acts out putting the key in the door and suddenly seeing MARLEY)

SCROOGE: Marley! Humbug!

NARRATOR: He paused, with a moment's irresolution, before he shut the door and double locked it.

It was an old house, cold and entirely cheerless in the interior, for nobody lived in it but Scrooge, who was farthest from warmth and cheer. He lit a pitifully small candle and groped toward his rooms.

(SCROOGE *changes into his robe and takes out the paper CRATCHIT gave him.*)

NARRATOR: He changed out of his dreary business clothes into his dressing gown. He sat down to light his fire and took out the pamphlet Bob Cratchit had given him. He was about to ignite it from his candle when he saw the words across the first page.

SCROOGE: (*Reading the title aloud*) "'Consider Your Ways, Saith the Lord.' Micah 5:2. (*Turns the page*) It is important that men think of their ways of life, for the Scriptures remind us that 'there is a way which seemeth right to a man, but the ends thereof are the ways of death.' Worldly gains and the riches of life are no security for eternity. As Christ said, 'What shall it profit a man if he should gain the whole world and lose his own soul?'

Therefore, let every man look to his past, his present, and his future and realize the need of true repentance before God. For those who trust in Christ will find forgiveness for the sins of the past, grace for victory in the present, and a home with Him in heaven in the future. Remember, 'believe on the Lord Jesus Christ and thou shalt be saved.'"

(SCROOGE *stops reading and mutters to himself as he puts the paper back into his pocket.*)

SCROOGE: ". . . Look to his past, his present, and his future," humbug! How cheeky of Cratchit to give this to me. I shall deal with him tomorrow—oh, it's Christmas tomorrow—well, the day after that I shall deal with him. What gall! "Consider thy ways!" Humbug!

NARRATOR: He sat in the dim firelight, troubled, bitter, and lonely on Christmas Eve, thinking over the past events of the day.

AUDIO CUE: Recorded Voices From Stave One

repeating what SCROOGE heard previously:

Audio C.S 1: Do I have the pleasure of addressing Mr.   Scrooge or Mr. Marley?

Audio SCROOGE: Marley's been dead these seven years. He died seven years ago this very night . . .

SCROOGE: *(Repeating to himself)* "Seven years ago this very night."

(SCROOGE looks toward where Marley's letter is)

NARRATOR: Suddenly, Scrooge remembered a letter he had never read. Unopened and ignored, it was a personal word written to him by Jacob Marley from his deathbed. Having Marley's will in hand and telling himself he had no time for sentimentality, Scrooge had long ago thrust the letter aside between two moldering volumes on the bookshelf, almost totally forgotten. Now the thought of that neglected correspondence began strangely bothering him.

SCROOGE: Humbug. *(He reaches for the letter.)*

NARRATOR: Scrooge drew the letter from its forsaken tomb. Dust stained it, and the paper had yellowed. He broke the seal and gazed on the page.

(SCROOGE looks over the paper. MARLEY prepares to enter.)

NARRATOR: There he saw the once familiar handwriting of Jacob Marley. The penmanship was shaky from the throes of death.

Scrooge began to read.

MUSIC: Piano plays tune of "A Christmas Plea To Sinners" *("I Wonder As I Wander" plays softly in the background, in a minor key if possible, as MARLEY speaks, coughing, wheezing, and gasping as he is near death)*

MARLEY: My dear Scrooge,

In life, I, Jacob Marley, was your partner. My life is now passing from me, and I must warn you to escape before it is too late, for I have been bound by my sin and only now, at the end, by God's grace, have I been freed.

I have worn the chains of sin and self-interest I forged in life. I made it link by link and yard by yard. I girded it on of my own free will, and of my own free will I wore it. Its pattern would not be strange to you, for in your deepest heart, you know the weight and length of the strong coil you bear yourself. It is a ponderous chain!

(With grief and lament) Why did I waste my life captive, bound, and double-ironed! With the deepest regret, I wish I could now make amends for the opportunities I misused in my life! But I have no such power left.

You may think to yourself that I was always a good man of business, but the souls of mankind were my business! Their spiritual welfare was my business! Charity, mercy, and forbearance in the gospel were all my business! The dealings of my trade were but a drop of water in the comprehensive ocean of my business. Why did I walk through the crowds of fellow beings with my eyes turned down, and only until here at the end to raise them to that blessed star which led the Wisemen to that poor little manger?

Hear me! I warn you that you have yet a chance and hope of escape. Do not put off receiving Christ as your Savior until the end, as I did. Death may come unexpectedly. I was almost too late, but God has been merciful to me. I implore you to forsake the path you now tread. The Lord will give you the grace to change.

Consider your ways, Ebenezer, and turn to the Savior while you may.

SCROOGE: *(Thoughtful, echoing both MARLEY and the gospel tract)* "Consider your ways."

MARLEY: *(Begins to exit)* My departure is at hand. You will see me no more unless we meet again at our blessed Savior's feet. Look that, for your own sake, you remember what has passed between us!

(MARLEY EXITS)

MUSIC: Out

NARRATOR: Scrooge set the letter aside and sat for a long time thinking. *(Pause)* At last, he grew drowsy, and sleep overcame him as he continued mulling over what had transpired that day.

MUSIC: Dream-like Piano music

AUDIO CUE: MORE RECORDED VOICES FROM STAVE ONE *(As SCROOGE begins to fall asleep)*

Audio FRED: I've always thought of Christmas as a good time; a loving, a kind, forgiving time—a reflection of God's heart toward us—a time for us to open our hearts toward Him.

Audio SCROOGE: I leave God alone, and I want Him to leave me alone.

Audio FRED: I'm going to pray that He does not leave you alone, especially at Christmastime.

Audio BOB: It's a gospel pamphlet. It tells how you can receive God's greatest gift, Salvation in Jesus Christ.

Audio MARLEY: Consider your ways, Ebenezer . . .

Audio SCROOGE: "Consider your ways, saith the Lord" past . . . present . . . future. . .

MUSIC: SOLO "A CHRISTMAS PLEA TO SINNERS" (Sung to the Melody from "I Wonder As I Wander")

A CHRISTMAS PLEA TO SINNERS

The Baby in the manger in old Bethlehem,
Was God's Son, Lord Jesus, the Savior of men.
The Shepherds, sent by Angels, to find Him that night,
In reverence and in wonder looked down at that sight.
This Child born of Mary grew into a man,
And suffered at Calv'ry to finish God's plan,
To pay our redemption, He hung on the cross,
That we might be rescued from infinite loss.
Your lifetime is fleeting, and soon will be o'er;
To you, He is pleading, "Come open the door."
To you, He is calling; for your soul He does cry;
For God is not willing that any should die.
For what will it profit, if you gain the world,
And then at the judgment into Hell you are hurled?
Dear sinner, are you ready? "Consider thy ways."
Turn to the Savior; give Him no more delay!

STAVE TWO: CHRISTMAS PAST

MUSIC: Westminster Chime Cycle sounds and strikes the hour at one o'clock.

NARRATOR: Scrooge continued in sleep, oblivious to the outside world, but in his slumber fretful thoughts began shaping dreams as he unconsciously looked to his past, his present, and his future. In his dream, he looked up. A young lady approached.

(SCROOGE looks up, FAN enters)

NARRATOR: A scene out of his past: he saw again his sister, Fan.

SCROOGE: Fan? Fan, is it you?

FAN: *(Softly, gently)* Ebenezer!

SCROOGE: Fan, I've missed you so.

FAN: Let us walk together and remember old times.

MUSIC: Dream-like Piano Music

(They move together)

SCROOGE: *(Clasping his hands together in excitement and surprise)* Fan, what is this? Can it be!? Remember this place? We were children here!

FAN: *(Smiling at him)* Let us go on. Remember the way?

SCROOGE: *(Eagerly)* Remember it? I could walk it blind folded!

AUDIO CUE: Sound of Country Lads passing by.

(The lads laugh and joke and wish each other a Merry Christmas.)

SCROOGE: (*Seeing the Lads*) Bless me! Look who's coming! It's Gilbert and his brother William, and Fred, Richard, John and (*trying to place the name*) . . . Percy, dear old Percy!

(*YOUNG SCROOGE enters. He is gloomy and unhappy at being left out and left behind.*)

MUSIC: Piano plays "Turn Your Eyes Upon Jesus" softly in background

FAN: (*Gesturing*) Look here. The school was not quite deserted. There you sat, a solitary young man, neglected by his friends.

SCROOGE: (*sadly*) I know it, but remember how you came to my rescue?

(*FAN and SCROOGE pause and gaze on the melancholy boy. A young girl suddenly rushes in, full of excitement. YOUNG SCROOGE can hardly believe that she has come to see him.*)

LITTLE FAN: (*Rushing in*) Ebenezer! Ebenezer! Oh, there you are, dear brother! Ebenezer, I've such wonderful news! I've come to bring you home, dear brother! (*She claps her hands*) To bring you home, <u>home</u>!

YOUNG SCROOGE: Home, little Fan?

LITTLE FAN: Yes! Home for good and all. Home, forever and ever. Father's so much kinder than he used to be. Now that he's received Christ, home is like heaven. (*Racing, running each phrase together in her excitement*) He spoke so gently to me one dear night when I was going to bed that I asked him again if you might come home; and he said, Yes, you should; and he sent me in a coach to bring you. And you're to be an apprentice! And never come back here; but first we're to be together all the Christmas long, and have the merriest time in all the world!

YOUNG SCROOGE: Home for good? Father's changed?

I . . . I can't believe it.

LITTLE FAN: Our pastor says it's the transforming power of Jesus Christ. Oh, how I wish for you to experience it for yourself. I hope you will someday.

YOUNG SCROOGE: If such a miracle has happened to father, I want to know more about it for myself.

LITTLE FAN: Come!

(*LITTLE FAN claps her hands with glee, and grabs YOUNG SCROOGE by the hand and eagerly leads him away. They exit Stage*

FAN: I was always a delicate creature whom a breath might have withered.

SCROOGE: But you had a large heart, so you had. I will not gainsay it.

FAN: I died a woman, and had a child.

SCROOGE: (*Stricken further*) One child.

FAN: My son—your nephew—Fred! (*Pause*) I died giving him birth.

MUSIC: Piano Out

SCROOGE: (*Ashamed and uneasy at the pangs on conscience*) Yes. I'm . . . I'm sorry. I've shunned Fred, blamed him for your death. How foolish I've been.

FAN: (*Gently taking him by the hand as if to show that she understands.*) Come, let us continue.

MUSIC: Dream-Like Piano Music

(*They move to the next scene from SCROOGE'S past*)

SCROOGE: (*looking up, amazed*) Oh, Fan! I always wanted to show you this place. I was apprenticed here!

(*The FEZZIWIGS enter, MR. FEZZIWIG rubbing his hands together in eager anticipation*)

SCROOGE: (*Crying out in great excitement*) Why, it's old Fezziwig! Bless my heart, it's old Fezziwig and dear Mrs. Fezziwig alive again! You'd have loved meeting them. The kindest people in the world!

MUSIC: Piano plays "Here We Come A Wassailing" softly in background.

MRS. FEZZIWIG: I believe it's time, dear.

FEZZIWIG: (*Takes out his pocket watch, glances at the time, and laughs*) You're right, my love, so it is. (*rubs his hands together again, and cries out in what Dickens called an "oily, rich, fat, comfortable voice"*) Yo ho, there! Ebenezer! Dick!

(*YOUNG SCROOGE and another young man, DICK, come running in*)

YOUNG SCROOGE and DICK: (*with slight bows to MRS. FEZZIWIG*) Evening, ma'am!

(*She smiles and bows back*)

SCROOGE: (*Excited*) It's Dick Wilkins, to be sure! Bless me, yes. He was very much attached to me, was Dick. Poor Dick! Dear, dear!

FEZZIWIG: Yo, ho, my boys! No more work tonight!. Christmas Eve, Dick! Christmas Eve, Ebenezer! Let's have those shutters up (*gives a sharp clap of the hands*) before a man can say "Jack Robinson!"

(*YOUNG SCROOGE and DICK run off stage*)

FEZZIWIG: Is everything ready, my dear?

MRS. FEZZIWIG: Everything's ready, and "you-know-who" just arrived

FEZZIWIG: I hope she strikes Young Ebenezer's fancy.

Mrs. Fezziwig: I know she will. (*Touches his hand, and confides in him with a knowing smile*) Woman's intuition, my dear.

NARRATOR: You wouldn't believe how those two fellows went at setting the shutters. They charged into the street with the shutters—one, two, three—had 'em in their places—four, five, six—barred 'em and pinned 'em—seven, eight, nine—and came back before you could have got to twelve, panting like race horses.

(*YOUNG EBENEZER and DICK dash back in*)

FEZZIWIG: Hilli-ho! (*Rubbing his hands*) Clear away, my lads! Let's have lots of room here! Hilli-ho, Dick! Hilli-ho, Ebenezer!

(*YOUNG EBENEZER and DICK quickly arrange the scene for the party*)

NARRATOR: There was nothing they wouldn't have cleared away

or couldn't have cleared away, with old Fezziwig looking on. And soon the guests began to arrive.

(ENSEMBLE *members begin to arrive during the following narration. This section of narration is long enough on purpose to allow the ensemble to come out on stage. It can be lengthened or shortened, if necessary*)

NARRATOR: In came the three Miss Fezziwigs, beaming and lovable. In came the stout young men from the warehouse, whose hearts they broke. In came all the men and women employed in the business. In they all came, one after another; some shyly, some boldly, some gracefully, some awkwardly; in they all came, any how and every how!

FEZZIWIG: (*Clapping his hands with glee*) Welcome! Welcome, my friends! Come, let us join together in song and rejoice in all the goodness the Lord has shown to us in this Christmas Season.

MUSIC: Fezziwig's guests sing "How Great My Joy" (*Or other joyful carol*)

(The ENSEMBLE *breaks up into small groups, conversing happily and slowly drifting out of the scene.*)

FEZZIWIG: (*Clapping his hands with glee*) Well done! Well done, everyone!

FAN: Mr. Fezziwig delights in making others happy.

SCROOGE: The happiness he gave was quite as great as if it cost a fortune. (*SCROOGE suddenly remembers his harsh treatment of Cratchit*)

FAN: Dear Brother, is something the matter?

SCROOGE: (*guilty pangs*) I should like to be able to say a word or two to my own clerk, Bob Cratchit just now.

FEZZIWIG: (*Calling*) Ebenezer! Ebenezer! Come here, my lad.

(*YOUNG SCROOGE comes to FEZZIWIG*)

FEZZIWIG: There is someone Mrs. Fezziwig and I have been wanting to introduce to you for a long time.

MUSIC: Piano plays "Barbara Allen" softly in the background.

(*MRS. FEZZIWIG brings BELLE over next to YOUNG SCROOGE*)

FEZZIWIG: Belle, I'd like to introduce you to Master Ebenezer Scrooge, the finest young financial mind in the city. Ebenezer, this is our niece, Belle.

BELLE: Pleased to meet you, Master Ebenezer.

(*YOUNG SCROOGE is speechless. He cannot take his eyes off her. He takes her hand to give it a light kiss, but does not release it. There is a moment of silence as the two gaze at each other with him holding her hand. (We usually had these two played by a married couple in real life, which brought a laugh on the next line.)*)

FEZZIWIG: (*Delighted*) Well, I'm glad you've finally met.

MRS. FEZZIWIG: Come along, dear.

(*YOUNG SCROOGE and BELLE freeze in place with him still holding her hand. The FEZZIWIGS exit*)

SCROOGE: Fan, there was another Christmas with this young woman I would you not see.

(*BELLE and YOUNG SCROOGE unfreeze. He drops her hand, and she turns away from him as she speaks.*)

MUSIC: Piano now makes a transition and plays

"I Wonder As I Wander" softly, slowly, sadly in the background.

BELLE: (*Softly, sadly*) It matters little. To you, very little. We do not serve the same God.

YOUNG SCROOGE: Nonsense, Belle. What can you mean?

BELLE: I've given my heart to Jesus Christ. You serve a different god, a Golden one.

YOUNG SCROOGE: You don't understand. The world is hard on poverty and condemns with severity the pursuit of wealth.

BELLE: You fear poverty too much. Your trust should be in God. What will it profit you if you gain the whole world and loose your own soul? Seek first God's kingdom, and He will add the rest that you need. I've seen your nobler aspirations fall off one by one until the master passion, Gain, engrosses you.

YOUNG SCROOGE: (*Defensive, because she has hit at his true heart*) What then? Even if I have grown so much wiser, what then? I'm not changed toward you.

(*She slowly shakes her head*)

BELLE: You are another man—but not the man you could have become when you talked of one day putting your faith in Christ. (*With resolve*) Our contract is an old one. Our engagement was made when we were both poor and content to be so. You <u>have</u> changed.

YOUNG SCROOGE: (*uncomfortable, grasping for an excuse*) I was a boy then.

BELLE: Your own feeling tells you what I say is true. That which promised happiness when we were one in heart is fraught with misery now that we are two. I've prayed keenly about this. I release you from your promise. I know now that we would be miserable together—unequally yoked.

YOUNG SCROOGE: Have I ever sought release?

BELLE: In words? No, never.

YOUNG SCROOGE: In what, then?

BELLE: In an altered spirit, in another atmosphere of life with another hope at its end. I release you, with a full heart, for the love of what him you once were and what you might become if you would receive Christ. (*Turning away with great sadness*) May you be happy in the life you've chosen.

(*BELLE walks slowly away, softly crying, dabbing at her nose with a handkerchief. YOUNG SCROOGE is speechless at first, he makes a hesitant move after her. He pauses until she is out the door and calls to her.*)

YOUNG SCROOGE: Belle, wait! I . . .

(*YOUNG SCROOGE pauses looking after her. Slowly his face grows dark as his heart turns bitter. He turns and briskly exits.*)

SCROOGE: (*Calling after his young self*) You fool! You young fool! Go after her! (*Grieved*) Oh, Fan! It hurt so much! It hurts me still!

(*SCROOGE begins to slowly retreat back to his chair*)

FAN: (*Gently admonishing him as he goes*) Dear brother, what you could have been if you had turned to Christ: Married to Belle as a faithful, Christian husband.

SCROOGE: (*Pained*) No!

FAN: Your home filled with happy, godly children.

SCROOGE: (*The truth hurting him*) No! Stop! Fan, please, I can't bear it! (*pleading*) Leave me, leave me.

MUSIC: Dream-like Piano Music as FAN exits

(FAN exits. Sobbing, SCROOGE sinks into the chair, his face in his hands, grieved at what has been revealed to him. He freezes in this position.)

STAVE THREE:
CHRISTMAS PRESENT

MUSIC CUE: WESTMINSTER CHIMES CYCLE sounding Two O'clock as CHARACTERS get in place for next scenes.

(SCROOGE is sleeping badly)

NARRATOR: Scrooge continued brooding in fitful slumber. His contemplations turned from his past to his present state. In his dream, someone vaguely familiar approached.

MUSIC: Dream-like Piano Music briefly to cover entrance of VENDOR

(SCROOGE slowly looks around as the VENDOR enters with a prodigious, friendly laugh.)

SCROOGE: I've seen you before . . . you . . .you're the chestnut vendor from last evening!

VENDOR: *(Laughing and jolly)* Come! Come n' know me better, man!

(SCROOGE slowly stands and looks with wonder and curiosity upon the VENDOR.)

VENDOR: *(Laughingly)* I can show you a Christmas the likes of which you've never seen before!

SCROOGE: I'm learning a lesson that is working now. If you've aught to teach me, let me profit by it.

MUSIC: More Dream-like Piano Music to cover change in location

(The VENDOR and SCROOGE journey to FRED and FELICIA'S party in progress)

SCROOGE: Where are we going?

FRED: Ha, ha, ha, ha, ha!

MUSIC: Piano Plays "The Holly And The Ivy"
softly in the background.

SCROOGE: *(Hearing the laughter)* Why, it's my nephew Fred, his wife, Felicia, and their gaggle of obnoxious friends. Must be the dinner party Fred tried to invite me to.

(SCROOGE shows much surprise and stares at FRED in wonder. FRED is in the midst of telling them a story and is overcome by his own laughter.)

FRED: Ha, ha, ha, ha, ha!

FELICIA, FRIENDS, and the VENDOR: Ha, ha, ha, ha, ha, ha!

FRED: *(As telling something humorous)* He said that Christmas was a "humbug," as I live! He believed it, too!

FELICIA: *(humorously shocked)* More shame for him, Fred!

FRED: He's a comical fellow. That's the truth, and not so pleasant as he might be. However, his offenses carry their own punishment. My mother loved him, and I try to, as well.

FELICIA: I'm sure he's wealthy, Fred. At least you always tell me so.

FRED: What of that, my dear? His wealth is of no use to him. He doesn't do any good with it. He doesn't even make himself comfortable with it. He hasn't even the satisfaction of thinking—ha, ha, ha!—that he's ever going to benefit us with it.

FELICIA: I've no patience with him.

(The OTHER LADIES murmur their agreement)

FRED: Oh, but I have! I'm very sorry for him. I couldn't be angry with him if I tried. Who suffers by his ill whims? Himself, always. He takes it into his head to dislike us, and he won't come and dine with us. What's the consequence? He loses some pleasant moments and pleasanter companions than he can find in his own thoughts, or in his moldy old office or dusty chambers. I mean to give him the same chance every year, whether he likes it or not, for I pity him.

(There is a thoughtful pause, and then FELICIA, sensing a serious turn in the festive mood, suggests a return to their enjoyment.)

FELICIA: Let's sing a song, Fred!

MUSIC: Fred's party guests sing "We Wish You A Merry Christmas" (or other Christmas song of the period)

FELICIA: Shall we play a game?

(EVERYONE agrees, some make suggestions: "A forfeit," "How, When, and Where," "Blindman's Bluff," etc. The VENDOR laughs with enjoyment.)

FELICIA: Let's play "Yes and No!" Fred, you be it first. *(To the others)* He's so clever at these things.

(EVERYONE agrees and calls on FRED to go first)

SCROOGE: *(Excited, forgetting he is merely an observer)* I haven't played that one for years.

FRED: Hmmm. All right, I think I've got a good one. Now, everyone remember I can only answer your questions with a 'Yes' or a 'No'—and that means you, Topper!

TOPPER: *(pretending to be indignant)* What? Me?!

(As the game progresses, FRED laughs to himself more and more at the clues. SCROOGE forgets they can't hear him and gives his input as well. The VENDOR laughs at each clue and at SCROOGE'S behavior. The lines for LADY and MAN could be split among the various other friends at the house.)

FELICIA: Is it an animal?

FRED: Hmmmm, Yes.

LADY: A live animal?

FRED: Yes.

TOPPER: Is it a pleasant animal or a disagreeable animal?

FELICIA: (Playfully scolding) Now, now! You must ask a "Yes" or "No" question!

SCROOGE: Follow the rules, young man!

TOPPER: Sorry. Is it a pleasant animal?

FRED: No.

SCROOGE: Ah, a somewhat disagreeable one!

MAN: Is it savage?

FRED: Yes.

LADY: Does it growl and grunt sometimes?

FRED: Yes.

SCROOGE: A noisy beast.

MAN: Does it walk about the streets of London?

FRED: Yes.

LADY: Oh, my, a savage animal out on the streets! Is it led by anyone?

FRED: No.

FELICIA: Does it live in a menagerie?

FRED: No.

LADY: Is it killed in a market?

FRED: No.

TOPPER: I know, I know! Is it a horse?

FRED: No.

SCROOGE: It must be some kind of wild beast.

LADY: A tiger?

FRED: No.

SCROOGE and TOPPER: A bear?

SCROOGE: I asked first!

FRED: No.

LADY: What can it be?

SCROOGE: Review the clues, madam: a live animal, somewhat disagreeable, on the streets, unled by anyone, not in a menagerie, nor killed in a market.

(Everyone is stumped, FRED is enjoying himself; FELICIA suddenly knows what it is.)

FELICIA: I know what it is! *(Mockingly scolding him)* Oh, Fred, you scoundrel!

FRED: What is it?

FELICIA: It's your Uncle Scro-oo-oge!

TOPPER: Uncle Scrooge?!

SCROOGE: *(Shocked)* Me?

FRED: *(Holding it in for dramatic effect and bursting out with laughter.)* Yes!

(Everyone laughs and laughs as SCROOGE watches and realizes how others perceive him.)

TOPPER: *(Pretending indignation again)* You should've answered "yes" when I asked, "Is it a bear?" You diverted my thoughts!

SCROOGE: *(Turning away from the party, speaking to himself)* Is this, then, how people perceive me? Am I really only an object of pity and humor rather than a respected man of business?

VENDOR: *(Laughing gently)* Come and know yourself better, Guv'ner. "Live and learn," that's what I always say. Come, another scene for you to see this day.

MUSIC: Dream-like Piano Music to cover

(SCROOGE and the VENDOR move to the next scene.)

SCROOGE: This is one of the run-down sections of the city. What can be in the midst of this poverty?

VENDOR: Yonder house, though small, poor and plain, holds abundant love and Christmas joy. Come and know it better.

SCROOGE: *(Suddenly realizing)* My! I know this place, though I've only been here a couple times before, bringing lace that needed washing. It's home to Bob Cratchit and his bothersome brood!

(The Ghost laughs at SCROOGE'S discovery)

(MRS. CRATCHIT enters, carrying a platter, and leading the YOUNGER CRATCHITS into the scene.)

MUSIC: Piano plays "We Gather Together To Ask The Lord's Blessing" or other hymn of Thanksgiving softly in the background.

MRS. C.: *(Concerned)* Where's your precious father, then? And your brother, Tiny Tim? And Martha warn't as late last Christmas Day by half an hour!

(MARTHA enters from Stage P.)

MARTHA: Here's Martha, mother!

MRS. C.: *(Greeting her daughter with a kiss)* My dear, how late you are!

MARTHA: We'd a deal of work to finish up last night and had to clear away this morning, mother.

MRS. C.: Well! Never mind, so long as you're come. Sit ye down before the fire and have a warm, Lord bless ye!

PETER: *(Seeing father approach)* No, no! Father's coming!

BELINDA: Hide, Martha, hide!

(MARTHA hides. The VENDOR laughs in enjoyment. BOB comes in cheerfully, playfully carrying TINY TIM, as if he were TINY TIM'S horse. TINY TIM holds a crutch.)

BOB: *(Looking around)* Why? Where's our Martha?

MRS. C.: Not coming.

BOB: Not coming! *(Losing his cheerful spirit)* Not coming upon Christmas Day?

MARTHA: *(Coming out of hiding)* Here I am, Father!

BOB: (Greeting MARTHA) Oh, Martha!

(CRATCHITS all laugh at the game and especially the VENDOR too, as

he watches)

PETER: *(Excited)* Come, Martha. See the pudding!

BELINDA: It's singing in the copper out in the washhouse.

(The CRATCHIT CHILDREN exit temporarily. MRS. C. makes final meal preparations as BOB talks.)

MRS. C.: And how did Tiny Tim behave?

BOB: As good as gold and better. Somehow, he gets thoughtful, sitting by himself so much. He told me, as we came home, that he hoped people would see him and it might be pleasant to them to remember, upon Christmas Day, *(tremulously)* who made lame beggars walk and blind men see. I do believe he's growing strong and hearty.

MRS. C.: *(Calling)* Come, children, everything's ready!

(CRATCHIT CHILDREN come back excitedly)

BOB: Gather 'round, my dears.

(MRS. C. carries the goose to the table.)

PETER, BELINDA, TIM: *(Pounding on the table)* The goose! The goose!

TIM: *(Feebly, coughing)* Hurrah!

SCROOGE: *(Shocked at the merger meal)* A merger goose for such a family as this.

BOB: *(Breathing in the scents)* Ah, there never was such a goose cooked in all England! May we bless Mr. Scrooge, the founder of our feast.

MRS. C.: *(Upset)* The "founder of the feast," indeed! I wish I had him here. I'd give him a piece of my mind to feast upon, and I hope he'd have a good appetite for it!

BOB: *(Trying to calm her)* My dear, the Children. Christmas Day!

MRS. C.: It should be Christmas Day, I'm sure, when one blesses such an odious, unfeeling man as Mr. Scrooge. *(Breaking into tears)* You know he is, Robert! Nobody knows better than you do, poor fellow!

BOB: *(Mildly, gently)* My dear, Christmas Day.

(MRS. C. dries her tears on her apron)

TIM: We should pray for Mr. Scrooge to get saved, shouldn't we, Father?

BOB: Yes, Tiny Tim, we should. Let us pray.

(The family holds hands around the table and bows in prayer. The VENDOR and SCROOGE both bow as well; SCROOGE does so awkwardly.)

BOB: Our heavenly Father, we remember this day one who is in desperate need of Your saving grace. On this day when we remember how You came to earth, we lift up in prayer the name of one You came to earth to save, Ebenezer Scrooge.

(SCROOGE looks up at the mention of his name and looks on in amazement at the remainder of the prayer)

BOB: Work in Mr. Scrooge's heart in some special way that he might see his need of salvation and come to you by faith. Bless now this food and our fellowship together. Amen.

OTHER CRATCHITS: Amen.

BOB: *(Happily looking around at his family)* A merry Christmas to us all, my dears. God bless us!

OTHER CRATCHITS: God bless us!

TIM: God bless us, every one!

(The VENDOR laughs a hearty laugh)

MUSIC: Piano out

SCROOGE: I wonder if Tiny Tim will live.

VENDOR: *(Becoming serious)* I think by next Christmas you'll see a vacant seat in the poor chimney corner, and a crutch without an owner, carefully preserved.

SCROOGE: *(pleading)* No, no! Oh, no, he must be spared!

VENDOR: *(with hardness, repeating SCROOGE'S words)* What then? If he be like to die, he had better do it "and decrease the surplus population."

(SCROOGE hangs his head, overcome by penitence and grief)

VENDOR: *(Putting his hand on SCROOGE'S shoulder, leading him away from the Cratchits.)* Man, forbear that wicked cant until you've discovered what the surplus is, and where it is. Will you decide what men shall live, and what men shall die? God is "not willing that any should perish," but that all might come to Him in repentance and faith.

SCROOGE: Have the Cratchits no refuge or resource to help poor Tiny Tim?

MUSIC: Dream-like Piano Music as VENDOR departs

VENDOR: *(Leading SCROOGE back to his chair as a bell sounds)* Are there no prisons? Are there no workhouses? *(As he says these lines, the VENDOR exits)*

STAVE FOUR: CHRISTMAS YET TO COME

MUSIC: Bell Sounds Three Times for Three O'Clock without Westminster Cycle

NARRATOR: As the clock sounded, Scrooge awoke, convicted by his own words. He remembered his troubled dream vividly and reflected on it.

SCROOGE: *(Talking to himself)* "Consider your ways . . . ." The past and the present have been before me, but what of that which is yet to come? *(Gravely)* I fear that more than anything, but as I now hope to live to be another man from what I was, I bear those thoughts as well.

NARRATOR: Scrooge sat a long time brooding and again fell into tormented slumber.

MUSIC: Dream-like Piano Music

(SCROOGE looks up from his chair to see the men talking)

MERCHANT 1: Old Scratch has got his own at last, hey?

MERCHANT 2: When did he die?

MERCHANT 1: Last night, I believe.

MERCHANT 2: Why, what was the matter with him? I thought he'd never die.

MERCHANT 1: *(With a yawn)* Who knows?

MERCHANT 2: What has he done with his money?

MERCHANT 1: I haven't heard. Left it to his company, perhaps. He hasn't left it to me. That's all I know.

(The MERCHANTS laugh)

MERCHANT 2: It's likely to be a cheap funeral. I don't know of anybody going to it.

MERCHANT 1: Suppose we make up a party and volunteer? I don't mind going if lunch is provided. *(Pats his stomach)* I must be fed, you know.

(They laugh again)

MERCHANT 2: Well, I never wear black gloves, and I never eat lunch, but I'll go if everybody else will. *(Stops for a thoughtful moment)* Come to think of it, I'm not at all sure that I wasn't his most particular friend, for we used to stop and speak whenever we met. Bye-bye!

(The MERCHANTS give their farewells and depart)

SCROOGE: *(Wondering about what he has seen)* I know those men. They're important businessmen in the city. Who could they be talking about?

MUSIC: Dream-like Piano Music

NOTE: The following scene with OLD JOE can be done with OLD JOE and MRS. DILBER speaking a simulated "Cockney" dialect. A version written that way appears in the Production Notes for this script.

(OLD JOE comes out first and is met by MRS. DILBER and the UNDERTAKER'S ASSISTANT carrying bundles of various sizes. ALL three cast glances around to make sure they are not being followed or observed.)

SCROOGE: These shabby people lurking about—one is my own charwoman—what mischief are they up to?

MRS. DILBER: *(Laughing to find they all arrived at the same place at the same time)* Look here, Joe, here's a chance! If it ain't the Undertaker's Assistant, and me, the charwoman, met here without meaning it!

(THEY all laugh or cackle)

OLD JOE: Ah, Mrs. Dilber, you couldn't have met in a better place! Come, come, my dears! Into the parlor a bit.

(THEY move together to another spot close by.)

MRS. DILBER: What odds, then? What odds? Every person has a right to take care of themselves. He always did! If he wanted to keep 'em after he was dead, the wicked old screw, why wasn't he natural in his lifetime? If he had been, he'd have had someone to look after him when he was struck with death, instead of lying gasping out his last there, alone by himself.

OLD JOE: It's the truest word that ever was spoke.

UNDERTAKER: *(Gravely)* It's a judgment on him.

OLD JOE: Who'll be first? Don't be shy, we're all friends here. Come on, show Old Joe what you've got.

(THEY look at each other, feeling a twinge of guilt, and are a bit hesitant about revealing what they have stolen.)

UNDERTAKER: *(Breaking the silence)* I'll go first, in the spirit of equanimity.

(The UNDERTAKER places a handkerchief or small sack in OLD JOE'S hands, and then takes out a small notebook and reads off a list of items as OLD JOE brings them out.)

UNDERTAKER: Wax seal, pencil case, pair of sleeve buttons, a brooch, dentures.

OLD JOE: *(Looking through it and appraising the value)* A pound, eight shillings and a sixpence on your account, and I wouldn't give another sixpence if I was to be boiled for not doing it. Now, what do you have, Mrs. Dilber?

(The UNDERTAKER is a bit disappointed. MRS. DILBER presents OLD JOE with a large bundle.)

MRS. DILBER: Here you go. *(She hands over a bundle for OLD JOE to look through)* Sheets and towels, two silver teaspoons, a pair of sugar tongs, and a pair of boots.

OLD JOE: *(Pulling something out)* What's this? Blankets? *(Holding them away)* His blankets?

MRS. DILBER: Whose else's do you think? He isn't likely to take cold without 'em, I dare say.

OLD JOE: He didn't die of anything catching? Eh?

MRS. DILBER: Don't be afraid of that. I ain't so fond of his company that I'd loiter about him for such things, if he did.

OLD JOE: *(Pulls out something long)* What do you call this? Bed-curtains?

MRS. DILBER: *(Laughingly in affirmation)* Bed-curtains!

OLD JOE: You mean to say you took 'em down, rings and all, with him lying there?

MRS. DILBER: Yes, I do. Why not?

OLD JOE: You were born to make your fortune, my dear. *(Looking in the bundle again, JOE pulls out a fine shirt)*

MRS. DILBER: You may look through that shirt till your eyes ache, but you won't find a hole in it, nor a threadbare place. It's the best he had. They'd have wasted it if it hadn't been for me.

OLD JOE: What do you mean, wasted?

MRS. DILBER: Putting it on him to be buried in, to be sure. Someone was fool enough to do it *(she glares at the UNDERTAKER)*, but I took it off again. If calico ain't good enough for such purpose, it ain't good enough for anything. It's quite as becoming to the body. He can't look any uglier than he did in that one.

(THEY all laugh)

OLD JOE: He frightened everyone away from him when he was alive, to profit us when he's dead!

(THEY laugh again and exit)

SCROOGE: *(Seated in his chair, talking to himself in his dream)* I see, I see. The case of this unhappy man might be my own. I shall not ignore its lesson. *(Concerned)* Is there not any person in this town who feels emotion caused by this man's death? I must see some tenderness connected with a death, or this darkness will be forever present in me.

MUSIC: Dream-like Piano Music

SCROOGE: *(Talking to himself in his dream, SCROOGE looks to the Cratchit's house.)* It's Bob Cratchit's house again.

MUSIC: Piano plays "What A Friend We Have In Jesus" in the background.

(The CRATCHIT CHILDREN sit solemnly by MRS. C., who is working with some cloth. PETER is reading out loud from the Bible.)

PETER: ". . . and He took a little child, and set him in the midst of them."

(MRS. C. suddenly puts her hands to her eyes in an effort to hide her tears. The children look at her with concern.)

MRS. C.: The color hurts my eyes. They're better now. It makes them weak by candlelight, and I won't show weak eyes to your father when he comes home. It must be near his time.

PETER: Past it, rather. I think he has walked a little slower than he used to, these last few evenings, Mother.

MRS. C.: *(Trying to be cheerful, but faltering)* I have know him walk with—I have known him walk with Tiny Tim upon his shoulder very fast indeed.

MARTHA: So have I, often.

PETER: So have I.

MRS. C.: But he was very light to carry and his father loved him so, that he was no trouble—no trouble. There is your father now!

(BOB enters and is greeted by MRS. C., who helps him off with his comforter. BOB sits slowly, and the children gather near to comfort him.)

MRS. C.: You were behind your time again today, dear.

BOB: I went by the place again. I had to. It looks so green. I wish you could have been with me, but we will walk there on Sunday. I promised him that we'd walk there on a Sunday. *(Begins to cry)* My little child! My little child! *(He regains his composure)* I'm sorry, my dears.

I met Mr. Scrooge's nephew, Mr. Fred, in the street today. He saw that I looked a little—just a little down, you know—and he inquired what had distressed me. He is the pleasantest spoken gentleman you ever heard, so I told him. His words were a great comfort to me, for with great kindness, he reminded me that because of our faith in Jesus Christ, we will be with Tiny Tim again someday!

MRS. C.: Amen.

CHILDREN: Amen.

MUSIC: Dream-like Piano Music

SCROOGE: *(Wondering to himself out loud)* Are these the shadows of things that will be, or are they shadows of things that may be only? Men's courses will foreshadow certain ends, to which, if persevered in, they must lead, but if the courses be departed from, the ends will change. But the change must be more than superficial. My heart itself must be changed. I must be truly transformed. It must be so, but who can help me change?

(Scene shifts to graveyard—see Production Notes)

MUSIC: Organ plays "I Wonder As I Wander" sadly, perhaps in a minor key, in the background.

(SCROOGE turns. He sees the name on the headstone—EBENEZER SCROOGE)

SCROOGE: *(Shocked)* NO! I was the dead man whom those businessmen spoke of! My curtains, my blankets, my shirt—my death was the one gloated over!

(SCROOGE sinks into his chair.)

SCROOGE: No! Oh, no, no! *(Calling, pleading)* Dear Lord! Help me! I don't want to be the man I've been. Help me change the shadows you showed me.

MUSIC: Bell Sounds Six Times for Six O'Clock without

NARRATOR: Scrooge awoke to the sound of the clock and his own voice.

SCROOGE: Do I face a Christ-less grave? Am I past all hope? What does the Bible say? *(looking around)*

NARRATOR: He found Marley's old Bible among the forgotten volumes on the bookshelf. He frantically scanned through the New Testament until his eyes came upon 2nd Corinthians, chapter five. Jacob Marley had underlined a verse in that chapter.

SCROOGE: What is this? *(Reading)* "If any man be in Christ, he is a new creature: old things are passed away; behold, all things are become new." *(Pause as his understanding is opened)* Now I understand! How suddenly clear! I can't change myself from the inside, but Jesus Christ can. It's what Little Fan told me about father. . . what Belle wanted me to see . . . what the Cratchits have that gives them comfort!

(SCROOGE falls on his knees, trembling with emotion)

Dear God! Thank you for melting this heart of stone. I am the greatest sinner in all England, and only Jesus Christ can save me. My greed was worthless. I understand Christmas now. I believe that the Lord Jesus came to be born in the manger, that He died on the cross in my place, and shed his blood for my sins. You are not willing that I should perish. O Lord, I turn now from my sin and receive Jesus Christ as my Savior. Change this wicked heart of mine and make me a new creature.

(Action continues right into the final STAVE)

STAVE FIVE: THE END OF IT

SCROOGE: *(Remains kneeling. He opens his eyes.)* The shadows of the things that would have been are gone.

MUSIC: Piano plays "Good Christian Men, Rejoice" softly, slowly in the background.

SCROOGE: *(In wonder)* The shadow of what I was is gone too! I'm a new creature! I have new life! *(Laughing and crying at the same time)* I don't know what to do! I'm as light as a feather! I'm as happy as an angel! I'm as merry as a school boy!

(Shouting out the window) Merry Christmas to everybody!

(A LAD enters as if on a Christmas errand)

SCROOGE: *(Seeing a passing LAD)* Ho there, my lad! What is to-day?

LAD: Eh?

SCROOGE: What is to-day, my fine fellow?

LAD: *(puzzled)* To-day? Why, Christmas Day!

SCROOGE: *(To himself)* It's Christmas Day! Praise the Lord, I haven't missed it! *(To the LAD)* Hallo, my fine fellow!

LAD: Hallo!

SCROOGE: Do you know the poulterer's, in the next street but one, at the corner?

LAD: I should hope I do!

SCROOGE: An intelligent boy! A remarkable boy! Have they sold the prize turkey hanging there? Not the little prize turkey, the great big one?

LAD: What, the one almost as big as me?

SCROOGE: What a delightful boy! It's a pleasure to talk with him. Yes, my buck!

LAD: It's hangin' there now.

SCROOGE: Is it? Go and buy it!

LAD: *(Thinking he's being pranked, starts to leave)* Walk-ER!

("Walker" was an expression from Victorian England meaning "Don't fool with me" or "You can't fool me.")

SCROOGE: No, no! I'm in earnest. Go and tell them to bring it here, that I may pay them and tell them where to deliver it. Come back with the man, and I'll give you a shilling. Come back with him in less than ten minutes, and I'll give you both half a crown!

LAD: *(Running off excitedly)* Whooosh!

SCROOGE: *(Rubbing his hands and laughing to himself)* I'll send it to Bob Cratchit's. He shan't know who sends it. It's twice the size of Tiny Tim!

(SCROOGE prepares himself and steps out as the narrator describes)

NARRATOR: Scrooge paid the lad and the poulterer, and sent the turkey on its way, and insisted on paying for a cab for them to carry it in, for it <u>was</u> a Turkey! He never could have stood upon his legs, that bird. He would have snapped 'em short off in a minute, like sticks of sealing wax.

Scrooge dressed himself "all in his best" and got out on the streets. Everywhere about him were the sights and sounds of Christmas.

(SCROOGE meets JOHN JENKINS.)

JENKINS: *(Humbly, nervously, with hat in hands)* Mister Scrooge, sir, excuse me, I've been looking all over for you. It's about my loan, sir.

SCROOGE: Oh, yes, Jenkins. A loan of forty pounds, I believe.

JENKINS: *(Trying to hand money to SCROOGE)* Scraped together what I could, sir, but please, I need more time, sir.

SCROOGE: I won't take it.

JENKINS: *(Thinking the worst)* Oh, please, sir! Don't send us to debtor's prison.

SCROOGE: Mr. Jenkins, I was very rude to you the other day. Please forgive me. I forgive you your debt of forty pounds. Keep what you have, and a Merry Christmas to you and your wife.

JENKINS: *(Amazed)* You <u>are</u> Mr. Ebenezer Scrooge, aren't you, sir?

MUSIC: Piano plays "Amazing Grace" softly in the background.

SCROOGE: *(Laughing)* But not the same one you saw the other day. God has done a work in my heart. I'm a new man now.

JENKINS: *(Overcome with joy)* Thank you, sir! *(Starting to run off)* Merry Christmas, sir, and God bless you!

SCROOGE: *(Calling after him)* He has, my good man! He surely has!

(SCROOGE turns to find the CHARITY SOLICITORS entering)

SCROOGE: *(Shaking their hands)* How do you do? I hope you succeeded yesterday. A Merry Christmas to you. I've been praying we'd meet again.

C.S. 1: *(Unsure)* Mr. Scrooge?

SCROOGE: Yes, that is my name, and I fear it may not be pleasant to you. Allow me to ask your pardon. And will you have the goodness to accept this bank draft? *(SCROOGE hands them a slip of paper.)*

C.S. 1: *(Looks at it, Surprised)* Bless you, sir!

C.S. 2: Mr. Scrooge, are you serious?

SCROOGE: If you please, not a farthing less. A great many back payments are included in it, I assure you.

C.S.1: *(Shaking his hands)* My dear sir, we don't know what to say to such munifi--

SCROOGE: *(Cutting the man off)* Don't say anything, please. God has done so much for me. Come and see me if you need more. Will you come and see me?

C.S. 1: We will. Merry Christmas to you!

C.S. 2: Merry Christmas!

SCROOGE: Thank you. I thank you fifty times. Bless you!

(The C.S.ES exit. The VENDOR enters.)

VENDOR: Chestnuts! Hot Chestnuts! *(Seeing SCROOGE and laughing)* Hello, Guv'ner! Got your Christmas Spirit today?

SCROOGE: *(Laughing with him)* I should say so, my good man! As you suggested, I "came" and now I "know it better!" I now know the true maker of Christmas joy, the Lord Jesus Christ.

(They both laugh, wish each other a Merry Christmas, and the VENDOR exits.)

MUSIC: Piano out

NARRATOR: Scrooge walked the streets, saluting everyone with tidings of the season. He found that everything could yield him pleasure.

He came at last to Fred and Felicia's church and stood outside watching the happy people enter.

(ENSEMBLE members enter carrying Bibles, come across, and "enter the church")

SCROOGE: *(Nervous, to himself)* I really should go in. I know I should. But it's been decades.

(FRED and FELICIA enter and begin to walk past SCOOGE, talking happily together, not noticing him there.)

SCROOGE: Fred! *(Takes his hands and gives them a hearty shake)* A Merry Christmas to you! A very Merry Christmas, my dear boy!

(FRED is shocked, and it takes him a while to gather his wits. FELICIA has never officially met SCROOGE.)

FRED: What?!

SCROOGE: I was praying I'd meet you here.

FRED: Praying?

SCROOGE: And this enchanting creature *(SCROOGE extends his hand and FELICIA places hers in his)*—I know this is your lovely wife, Felicia. *(He kisses her hand)*

(FELICIA is charmed by SCROOGE and his compliments)

FELICIA: *(Her hand still in his)* Oh, Fred, who's this delightful gentleman?

FRED: *(Perplexed)* This . . . um, "delightful gentleman" is my Uncle . . . Ebenezer Scrooge!

(FELICIA quickly drops her hand as if she's touched something awful, and

steps back, repulsed by who she thinks she is meeting)

FRED: At least, I think it's my Uncle Scrooge.

SCROOGE: Oh, not the old Uncle Scrooge, Fred. The new one. Born-again this morning!

FRED: Born-again? You mean . . .

SCROOGE: Yes! The Lord convicted my cold, bitter heart about what you and others have said to me about Jesus Christ. This morning, I prayed for Him to save this covetous, old, wicked sinner, and He made me a new creature. I'm saved, Fred. Saved from my sin through the Son of God!

FRED: *(Shaking his hands, FELICIA joining in)* Amen!

FELICIA: This is the most wonderful answer to prayer!

FRED: Are you coming in to church?

SCROOGE: I want to, but it's been so long. I'm not sure how to go about it.

FELICIA: Come in with us, then.

FRED: We have a fine preacher, and the music is wonderful.

FELICIA: And afterwards, you must come home with us to dinner!

SCROOGE: May I still come?

FRED: Of course! And would you tell all our friends what God has done for you?

SCROOGE: Gladly!

FELICIA: It'll be the best Christmas for everyone!

(FRED locks one arm with SCROOGE'S, FELICIA locks with the other arm, and SCROOGE, FRED, and FELICIA exit together.)

AUDIO CUE: RECORDING OF CONGREGATION SINGING

"HARK THE HERALD ANGELS SING" Music fades out as SCROOGE, FRED, AND FELICIA "enter the church."

NARRATOR: Scrooge entered that local church, and for the first time in his life experienced the joy of singing with other believers in praise to God.

MUSIC: Bell Sounds Nine Times for Nine O'Clock
without Westminster Cycle

(SCROOGE enters during the chimes and goes quickly to his office)

NARRATOR: Scrooge arrived early at the office the next morning. Oh, he was early there! If he could only be there first and catch Bob Cratchit coming in late! He set his heart on it!

The clock struck nine. No Bob.

A quarter past. No Bob.

(BOB enters quietly, sneaking in.)

NARRATOR: He was a full eighteen and a half minutes behind his time.

(BOB sits down and begins working furiously away as if he could catch up with his lost time.)

SCROOGE: What do you mean by coming here at this time of day?

BOB: I'm very sorry, sir. I am behind my time.

SCROOGE: Yes, I think you are. Step this way, sir, if you please.

BOB: *(Pleading)* It's only once a year, sir. It shall not be repeated. I was making rather merry yesterday, sir.

SCROOGE: *(With pretended seriousness)* Indeed? Now, I'll tell you what, sir. I'll not stand for this sort of thing any longer. And therefore *(He approaches BOB, who is trembling, fears he's about to be fired. SCROOGE can't keep a straight face and begins to laugh)* . . . and therefore, I'm about to <u>raise</u> your salary.

BOB: *(Perplexed)* Are you all right, sir?

SCROOGE: A Merry Christmas, Bob! I'm more right than I've ever been. I read that gospel pamphlet you gave me. I trusted the Lord Jesus as my Savior. He's changed my heart. A Merrier Christmas, my good fellow, than I've given you for many a year!

BOB: Praise the Lord! We were praying for you just the other day.

SCROOGE: Somehow I knew you would. Your prayers have been answered, Bob.

BOB: God has been good!

SCROOGE: He has, Bob, and He will help me do good for you. I'll raise your salary and assist your struggling family. We shall discuss your affairs this very afternoon over lunch, Bob! Make up the fires, and buy another coal scuttle before you dot another *i*, Bob Cratchit!

(BOB CRATCHIT exits quickly. SCROOGE remains through the final narration.)

<u>EPILOGUE</u>

MUSIC: Piano plays "I Wonder As I Wander" softly in the background during the final narration.

(NARRATOR steps from his stool and stands beside SCROOGE)

NARRATOR: Scrooge was better than his word. By God's grace, he did it all, and the Lord did infinitely more. And to Tiny Tim— (*Pausing as TINY TIM runs to SCROOGE, who picks TINY TIM up*) who did <u>NOT</u> die— Scrooge was a second father. He became as good a friend, as good a master, and as good a Christian as the good old city knew. Some people laughed to see the alteration in him, but he let them laugh, and his own heart laughed with them. He knew WHO had changed him, and freely told everyone about it.

(*Contemplatively*) It was always said of Scrooge that he knew how to keep Christmas well, if any man alive possessed the knowledge. He had truly been transformed through faith in Jesus Christ. May <u>that</u> be said of us, and all of us. (*Turns toward TINY TIM*) And so, as Tiny Tim observed,

TINY TIM: (*Very loud, so everyone can hear*) God Bless Us, Every One!

(*The other CHARACTERS come out on stage and sing with the choir. The Congregation joins in on the last verse.*)

MUSIC: CHARACTERS, CHOIR, AND CONGREGATION SING "JOY TO THE WORLD"

The End

INVITATION

PRODUCTION NOTES
For "A CHRISTMAS CAROL"

Suggested Cockney-like Dialect for Pawn Broker's Scene:

(*UNDERTAKER'S ASSISTANT does not use the dialect*)

MRS. DILBER: (*Laughing to find they all arrived at the same place at the same time*) Look 'ere, Joe, 'ere's a chance! H'if h'it h'ain't the Undertaker's Assistant, an' me, the charwoman, met 'ere wiffout meaning h'it!

(*THEY all laugh*)

OLD JOE: Ah, Mrs. Dilber, you couldn't 'ave met h'in a betta place! Come, come, me dears! Inta the parlor a bit.

(*THEY move together slightly to an another spot close by.*)

MRS. DILBER: What odds, then? What odds? H'every person 'as a royght ta take care o' themselves. 'Ee always did! If 'e wanted ta keep 'em h'after 'ee was dead, the wicked old screw, why wasn't 'e natural h'in 'is lifetime? If 'ee 'ad been, 'e'd 'ave 'ad someone ta look h'after 'im when 'ee was struck wiff death, h'instead o' loin' gasping h'out 'is last there, h'alone boy 'imself.

OLD JOE: H'it's the truest word whut h'ever wus spoke.

UNDERTAKER: (*Gravely*) It's a judgment on 'im.

OLD JOE: Hoo'll be first? Don't be shy, we're h'all friends 'ere. Come own, show H'old Joe whut yew've got.

(*THEY look at each other and all feel a twinge of guilt and are a bit hesitant at revealing what they have stolen.*)

UNDERTAKER: (*Breaking the silence*) I'll go first, in the spirit of equanimity.

(The UNDERTAKER places a handkerchief or small sack in OLD JOE'S hands, and then takes out a small notebook and reads off a list of items as OLD JOE brings them out.)

UNDERTAKER: Wax seal, pencil case, pair of sleeve buttons, a brooch, dentures.

OLD JOE: (*Looking through it* and appraising the value) Tew pounds, h'eight shillings h'and a sixpence h'on yer account, h'and Oy wouldn't give 'nother sixpence, if Oy wus ta be boiled for not doin' h'it. Now, whut da yew ave, Mrs. Dilber?

(The UNDERTAKER is a bit disappointed. MRS. DILBER presents OLD JOE with a large bundle.)

MRS. DILBER: 'Ere ya go. (*She hands over a large bundle for OLD JOE to look through*) Sheets 'n towels, two silver teaspoons, pair o' sugar tongs, and h'a pair o' boots.

OLD JOE: (Pulling something out) Whut's this? Blankets? (*Holding them away*) 'Is blankets?

MRS. DILBER: Oose else's do ya think? 'Ee hain't loikely ta take cold wiffout 'em, Oy dare say.

OLD JOE: 'Ee didn't doy of anything catchin'? Eh?

MRS. DILBER: Don't be afraid o' that. Oy ain't so fond o' 'is company that Oy'd loiter h'about 'im fer such things, h'if 'ee did!

OLD JOE: (*Pulls out something long*) What do ya call this? Bed-curtains?

MRS. DILBER: (*Laughingly in affirmation*) Bed-curtains!

OLD JOE: Yew mean to say yew took 'em down, rings h'and h'all, wiff 'im lying there?

MRS. DILBER: Yes, Oy do. Whoy not?

OLD JOE: Yew were born ta make yer fortune, me dear. (*Looking in the bundle again, JOE pulls out a fine shirt*)

MRS. DILBER: Ya may look through that shirt 'till yer eyes ache, but yew won't find an 'ole in it, nor a threadbare place. H'it's the best 'ee 'ad. They'd have wasted h'it, h'if h'it 'adn't been fer me.

OLD JOE: Whutta ya mean 'wasted?'

MRS. DILBER: Puttin' h'it on 'im ta be buried in, ta be sure. Someone wus fool enough ta do h'it (*she glares at the UNDERTAKER*), but Oi took h'it off again. H'if calico h'ain't good enough fer such purpose, it ain't good enough fer anything. H'it's quite as becoming ta the body. Ee can't look any uglier than 'ee did h'in that one.

(*THEY all laugh*)

OLD JOE: He frightened everyone away from him when ee wus h'aloyve, to profit us when Ee's dead!

****

MUSIC
Here is a list of suggested music. Besides the Choir, a smaller Ensemble can be used in some places. There is a place for a vocal solo. The Piano and organ also plays softly in the background in designated places.

"O Come, All Ye Faithful" Choir Entrance, if used

In the Drama:

"O Come, O Come, Immanuel" Choir

"Caroling, Caroling" Ensemble

"I Wonder As I Wander" ("A Christmas Plea To Sinners")
Solo (and Piano)

"Turn Your Eyes Upon Jesus" (Piano)

"How Great My Joy" Ensemble

"Here We Come A Wassailing" (Piano)

"Barbara Allen" (a folk song) (Piano)

"We Wish You A Merry Christmas" Ensemble

"The Holly And The Ivy" (Piano)

"We Gather Together To Ask The Lord's Blessing" (Piano)

"What A Friend We Have In Jesus" (Piano)

"Amazing Grace" (Piano)

"Good Christian Men Rejoice" (Piano)

"Hark the Herald Angels Sing" (recorded, see below)

"Joy to the World" Choir, Cast and Congregation

Suggested Pre-Recorded Audio
Recording of Voices from Stave One

Recording of Country Lads passing by

Recording of a Church Congregation singing "Hark The Herald
Angels Sing"

The Importance of Spectacle

For centuries, going back to Aristotle, **Spectacle** has been an essential element in dramatic production. This encompasses visual and audio elements, such as staging, sets, costumes, lighting, and special effects. It is key facet in creating an engaging and entertaining audience experience.

STAGING

We performed this on in our church in an open stage with minimum furniture. We used the front of our platform, the steps leading up to it, and the auditorium floor level in front of the platform. We had a central baptistery above and behind the choir and used that too (see below). The pulpit and regular service furniture were cleared away. A lot of our main platform area was taken up by our expanded orchestra, but we had some portable platforms to make a small "thrust stage" performance area extending the platform at the front.

The entire platform and choir area were decorated with Christmas lights, garlands and wreaths. We had some Victorian-looking street lamps and set some Victorian-looking store fronts across the walls behind the choir.

We used a minimum of furniture: A sign hanging from a post saying "Scrooge & Marley." A coat rack. A small wooden table and chair for BOB CRATCHIT'S desk, a stand up desk for SCROOGE'S office. A wing-backed chair for SCROOGE to sit in and sleep in at home. A table and chairs for the CRATCHIT FAMILY home. A tombstone reading "Ebenezer Scrooge" for the graveyard.

We utilized our Baptistery as a special alcove for the Marley's Letter Scene and for the Graveyard Scene. We covered the water tank with a platform. We set a chair out for MARLEY and replaced it later with a tombstone for the graveyard. We highlighted the graveyard using ultraviolet black lights. We created "ground fog" by putting dry ice into buckets of warm water. The resulting "fog" (heavier than air) flowed around the tombstone and down out of the baptistery opening.

COSTUMING

We dressed up all our actors and members of the choir as well in a simple Victorian style (not exact period costumes, but giving the flavor).

Ladies wore bonnets, mop caps, long dark skirts and shawls, white blouses, pinafores, aprons, dark stockings and shoes.

For the men, skilled-at-sewing folks from our church sewed capes and altered coat lapels on used garments purchased at resale shops. The men wore waistcoats, cummerbunds, and suspenders. Collars on mens' shirts were replaced and turned up. Cravats were worn or neck ties were made from ribbon. A long scarf or muffler gave the impression of colder weather in some scenes. We bought some plastic top hats for the men.

There is other information On Line and from the public library about adapting and altering modern garments to give a simple "Victorian Look." An On Line search for "adapting clothing for Victorian costumes" will turn up helpful articles and videos.

We also had the benefit of renting more elaborate costumes from a Bible college for some of the main characters. The Academy of Arts' Logos Theatre in Taylors, SC also offers a rental service for certain costumes and props including "Christmas Carol" costumes from their own productions. First come, first served. (They have odd working hours due to any on-going productions and are often closed on Sundays and Mondays, so check their website for specifics.) https://rentals.thelogostheatre.com Email rentals@TheAcademyOfArts.org or call 864.268.9342.

COVERING SCENE CHANGES WITH CHIMES

We used the sounds of the Westminster Chime Cycle to cover for our scene changes with stagehands (dressed in black) and characters moving in and out in our open staging situation. These chimes also indicated the progression of time in the story as SCROOGE journeys through past, present, and future in his troubled sleep.

The Chimes usually sounded through a complete cycle, four notes for each quarter hour, followed by low chime for the bell sounding each particular hour—one for one o'clock, two for two o'clock; three for three o'clock, etc., covering the interval while actors and scene changers set up and take down as necessary between scenes. We owned a set of chrome concert chimes for our orchestra, but recorded chimes will work as well.

USING MEMBERS OF THE CHOIR IN THE DRAMA

Like many churches, some of our better actors are all ready involved in the choir. Rather than take them away from that for the entire drama, we had the ones portraying characters temporarily leave and return. These actors, along with the rest of the choir, were already in costume, so they stepped out from the choir area during the Westminster Chime Cycles, performed their particular scenes, and returned to their choir seats during the next cycle. The same thing for the Ensemble performing as FRED'S FRIENDS and as FEZZIWIG'S GUESTS. Choir members enjoyed the opportunity of being a part of the drama as well as singing. The congregation enjoyed seeing more of the people they knew involved as well.

As mentioned before, at the beginning of our program, we had the choir enter from the rear of the auditorium singing "O Come, All Ye Faithful" while holding battery-operated candles. This was different and added to the aspect of Spectacle in our production.

LIGHTING

We were located near Milwaukee, WI and rented a basic stage lighting set and dimmer board from a local theatrical supply company to supplement our regular auditorium stage lighting. We also used flood lights, black light bulbs, and clip-on utility lights purchased from a hardware store and Walmart.

TIPS FOR ACTORS

Here are some fundamental principles to concentrate on. I have learned over the years to concentrate on these when working with amateur actors in church and school productions. Even if you have never had training or experience in drama, if you will focus on these areas, they will go a long way into making your part in a production a success.

MEMORIZE

Nothing makes a production go smoother than having the lines and cues thoroughly memorized. An audience feels uncomfortable when there are awkward pauses because someone has forgotten a line.

The <u>minimum performance of a role</u> in an amatuer production involves 1) thoroughly memorized lines which are 2) spoken loud enough for everyone in the audience to hear.

Although these productions may be done in a modified Readers Theatre style, this does not mean that the characters actually *read* from their scripts. The word *Readers* in the term *Readers Theatre* refers to the storytelling quality of the drama rather than the actors' method of delivery. Even our narrators should have their lines memorized. They may hold their scripts in black choir folders partly as a prop to enhance the storytelling aspect of their narration, and partly to be able to prompt themselves or one of the characters if a line was missed.

MEMORY TAKES TIME AND COMMITMENT

Memorization will take commitment from your actors. It will require you to check up on their progress by setting deadlines. Memorization is work—dull, boring work—and takes time. Lines must be drilled and drilled and drilled until they are word perfect and on cue. One reason the word "rehearsal" is used for practice time is that it is necessary to "re-hear" the drama, over and over, to thoroughly learn it for performance. When faced with learning a difficult line, I will often drill myself 25 times or more with that line out loud to "program" my brain and the "muscle memory" used by my voice, my lips, and my tongue in how it should be said.

PROGRAM THE MIND

Memorization also does something else important. It frees part of the brain now to think about how something is said rather than worrying on what to say next. When you learn something for the first time, in acting or any other activity, it usually takes your total concentration to do it. After you practice or memorize a task you will find that you don't have to place as much mental focus on what you are doing. It becomes automatic as you have "programmed" yourself to do it.

Again, after thoroughly memorizing their lines, actors will now liberate part of their brain to think on the interpretation of their lines, rather than merely reciting them. Interpretation includes vocal inflection and volume, hand gestures, facial expression, and body posture. In summary, memorization gives freedom in *how* something is said rather merely *what* is to be said.

PRACTICE WITH A RECORDING

Years ago, I would record a script on a tape recorder saying the other characters' lines and leave a silent space for my lines. I would play that recording over and over, at home while doing the dishes, in the car, at work (if possible), etc., learning the cue lines along with saying my own. I still make audio recordings like this to this day using my phone or other device.

"GET THE TRAIN ON THE TRACK"

Even the most thoroughly prepared actors may stumble, forget a line, or be distracted before a live audience. If this happens, work to get the story right back "on track" and keep going. I tell my actors that we are the only ones who know how something was supposed to be said or done, and the audience will not usually know when someone was covering for someone else's slip-up. "Get the train back on the track," and keep the story moving along as much as possible back in the right direction.

SPEED

A word of caution: When people memorize something they tend to speed up when they recite it back (like kids often do when they recite Bible verses.) Be sure to warn your actors to slow down if necessary, especially when they are nervous before a live audience. The audience is hearing and seeing everything for the first time and needs to mentally and emotionally digest what is going on, so caution the actors to watch their pace.

VOLUME

It does not matter how well an actor has his lines down or how well developed he is in his characterization if the audience cannot hear him. Microphones are not always practical to use, so the actors must learn to project their voices to the rear of the auditorium. I tell my actors to pretend that there is an elderly lady sitting in the back row who is hard of hearing, so they must speak slow enough and clearly enough so she can hear.

USING THE BODY

Encourage your actors to use more than their voices. Tell them to practice in front of a mirror working on facial expressions and hand gestures. Have them think about how they stand or sit to reflect how their character feels. Tell them to get their hands up above their waistlines when gesturing so the audience can see the use of the hands.

USING THE EYES

Shakespeare says, "the eyes are the window of the soul." An actor's eyes are very important in showing his emotional actions and reactions.

If your production uses a traditional staging with actors interacting with each other, characters should make regular eye contact with anyone speaking directly to them and with anyone their character speaks to. Also they should use their eyes to show the thought process behind what their character is saying or in reaction to what someone else is saying. Using the eyes helps a lot to give depth and believability to a characterization.

FIXED FOCUS IN READERS THEATRE

In Readers Theatre staging, since the actors do not usually face each other as in a traditional stage production. They have a "fixed focus," a point in space they look at out toward the audience, as if they are looking into the face of the one they may be talking to or hearing. The lines of focus should all intersect out in space. It is often helpful for the actors to pick a spot on up the back wall, a clock or some other "target" to aim at for their "focus." This will help them be consistent in the way they deliver their lines. It will also may help them in raising their faces, in speaking out over the audience to the back of the room. Nervous actors often hold their heads down, afraid to look toward the audience. They need to keep their faces up, so people can see their expressions and better hear their lines. Instead of looking at people in the audience, if that is distracting, they may look just above the audience's heads, (all the way to the back of the main floor).

THINK ABOUT THE CHARACTERS

The craft of acting is a lot about "pretending." Just like a child does while playing at "Cops and Robbers, House, or Cowboys and Indians," an actor pretends to be someone else, only on a deeper level. Actors should think about their character. Who are they supposed to be? How old are they? How do they walk and talk? Do some research if necessary. The ancient Greek word for an actor is the root word for *hypocrite*. It is a compound word formed from words meaning "under" and "to judge." The Greeks wore masks in their drama performances. The actors "judged" who they were "under" the mask. Modern actors pretend on the outside, judging on the inside who their character ares and how they talk and act.

SELF REHEARSAL

In addition to group times, everyone must practice on their own. They will be better prepared if they do not rely on group rehearsal time alone to develop their parts. Tell them to practice in front of a mirror and see how they look. Are they communicating what they want to communicate? Tell them to work at raising their part to a new level each time their rehearse.

TRANSITIONS

Drill your cast, choir, and musicians to make quick, smooth transitions from acting to music and from music to acting. Have any movement (up and down, on and off stage, in and out, etc.) pre-arranged and practiced so that everything flows from one area to another. Work to avoid awkward pauses as everyone waits for someone to get into place or for a light or sound cue to happen. This will help keep the audience's attention and empathy focused on the performance and not on their wrist watches or cell phones. It sometimes helps to have "walk on music" or "walk off music," a theme song or a bit of the previous song, to cover for a longer transition.

A reminder: If you produce any of these dramas in your church, school or organization, please notify the author and let him know how things went. You may e-mail him at pilz.author@gmail.com.

God Bless You In Your Production!

About the Author

Randy Pilz is the father of five wonderful children and, at this writing, proud grandfather of nine precious grandchildren.

Born and raised in the Chicagoland area, Randy trusted in Jesus Christ as his Savior through a community Bible study during his junior year in high school (the character Joe Anderson's testimony in Randy's first drama, "The Greatest Love," is partly based on Randy's real testimony). After salvation, the Lord led him to Bob Jones University, where he studied Bible, Speech and Drama.

With a heart for Christian service, Randy taught in two different Christian schools in Wisconsin. He later became drama director at Falls Baptist Church in Menomonee Falls, Wis. Through that ministry he began writing plays and programs as tools for local church evangelism.

For eleven years, Randy then served as a Creative Director/Video Producer on the staff at Pensacola Christian College, producing promotional and educational videos and assisting in the production of the *Rejoice in the Lord* telecast. He later worked as an independent producer in a non-profit media ministry.

In the fall of 2016, Randy began his third "tour of duty" as a Christian school teacher, instructing Junior and Senior High Students at Mountain View Baptist School in the Birmingham, AL area.

In the summer of 2020, health concerns brought Randy to relocate the Greenville area in South Carolina close to some of his children and grandchildren.

Six of his Christmas and Easter dramas have been novelized and are available at Amazon.com.

He has plans to write other plays and novels in the future as the Lord gives him time and energy.

You may contact the Randy at pilz.author@gmail.com

Acknowledgments

Special thanks to the people and pastoral leadership at Falls Baptist Church in Menomonee Falls, WI where these dramas were first written and produced as part of evangelistic Christmas outreaches during 1990s.